RAISING ANGORA RABBITS AND USING THEIR WOOL

A guide to my experiences raising angora rabbits and to creating warm and beautiful apparel from their wool.

MARIA K LINDBERG

Copyright © 2024 by Maria K. Lindberg

ISBN: 979-8-89694-464-5 - Ebook
ISBN: 979-8-89694-465-2 - Paperback
ISBN: 979-8-89694-466-9 - Hardcover

Printed in the United States of America

www.Oakknollangoras.com

About the illustrations and photos in this book:

Maria Lindberg provided many of her own sketches. Photos were taken throughout the years by our dad, Peter Lindberg, as well as those contributed by family members and friends in and around Blue Earth, Minnesota. Grandson Micah Lindberg contributed sketches inspired by his experiences with Grandma and her bunnies.

All graphics and images are the work of the above, except where attribution and permission of others is indicated.

Mike Lindberg

August 2024

CONTENTS

INTRODUCTION

Hello. I am Maria Lindberg, a long-time angora rabbit enthusiast. Here in Blue Earth, Minnesota, I am frequently called the "bunny Lady". I suppose that is appropriate since I welcome opportunities to demonstrate, with a rabbit on my lap, the spinning of that rabbit's wool. It gives me a platform from which I can, in an area with serious winters, talk about the unique properties of angora fiber. It is much warmer than wool, very lightweight and wonderfully soft. In America, it is usually regarded as a luxury fiber, but in Europe it is prized for its warmth. It is the warmth that I emphasize.

A Bit of History

In the photo on the next page, I am the older girl. I was named after my grandmothers, Maria and Sophia. My sister, Elna Pauline, was named after her mother and father.

My father at the time was the pastor of St. Peter's Lutheran Church, four miles west of Pender, Nebraska. His parents had him named Paul Franz Karl Kuehner, but he signed his name Paul C Kuehner because it was quicker to write. My mother was called Mrs. Paul Kuehner, but she reminded people frequently that her name was Elna Bothilde Peterson Kuehner.

In this photograph, we are all standing in front of the home (presumably) of one of my father's parishioners. We had probably been invited for Sunday dinner. The young dog in the picture had just dug up a dead chicken.

This preceding photo apparently was taken in the late 1930s. At that time, angora rabbit hair garments were quite popular. I had a fluffy white headband which tied under the chin, it was called a "Gibber".

I also had a short-sleeved jacket with fancy buttons and which had been dyed a peach color.

I remember, too, that angora hair of #1 quality was worth commercially about eleven dollars a pound. I was about ten, and I must have convinced my father that I'd make a lot of money if I could raise angora rabbits: at any rate, he bought three young French angoras for me - a buck and two does. They produced young - and hair - but I did not take good care of them, and did not sell any wool. Mats were worth fifty cents a pound, not enough to pay for postage. I don't know how long I had these animals - perhaps three years - but I liked them, and thought occasionally about raising them again.

(Fast forward to 1981) Married, with children, we had moved to a small farm on the edge of Blue Earth, MN.

At the Martin County Fair in nearby Fairmont, MN, I happened upon an exhibit of Corinne Pearson's angora rabbits. Delighted, I made a visit to her rabbitry and purchased a young buck and two does.

It wasn't very long before I had a lot of rabbits - and a lot of wool. What was I to do with all of that lovely fiber that keeps growing year-round?

As an adult, I did a better job of caring for the animals and their hair. I sold some raw fiber, but soon realized that there was more demand for finished products. The next logical step, then, was to learn how to spin.

My husband, Pete, always eager to make mechanical things from scrap, fashioned an electric spinner for me using a salvaged motor and treadle. It had two speeds - one fast, and one not quite so fast.

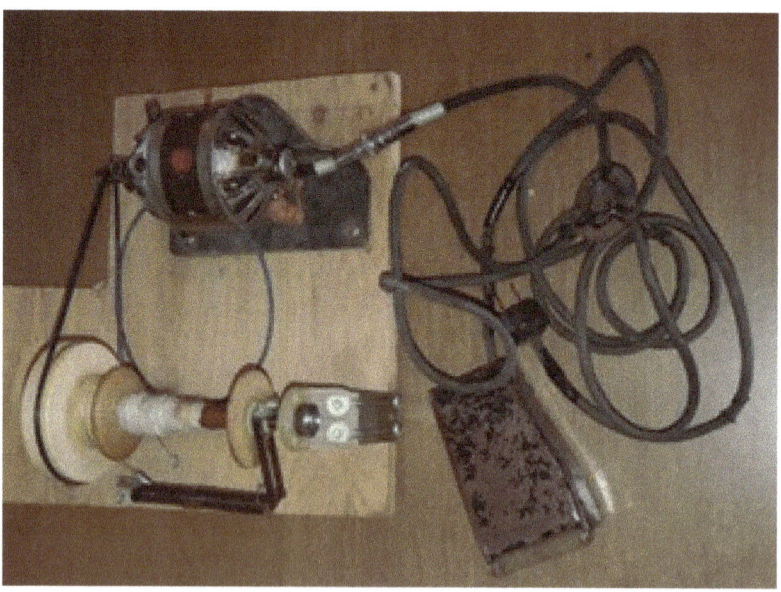

Without variable speed, I was constantly re-threading.

At the end of a year of working at it, I had one-third of an ounce of single-ply yarn. My daughter Lisa, who spins sheep wool said, "Mom, get yourself a decent wheel!!"

Chagrined, perhaps, that his invention wasn't a 'decent wheel', husband Pete put together my new Ashford.

I found out that I didn't need more practice. I had the basics down. I could spin!

Figure: A new Ashford spinning wheel. Image used with permission of the manufacturer.

ABOUT THIS BOOK

This book is a distillation of my forty years' experience with my French angora rabbits.

I've always had cold feet. Perhaps walking to Rural School Number 4 in northeast Nebraska winters was my start of what we called chilblains. (That word is in the Webster's dictionary.)

It wasn't until years later when I started working with angora fiber that I first experienced the incredible warmth that angora can provide for hands and feet.

My husband Pete and I married in 1954. Our country was then involved in the Korean war, and young men eligible for military service were drafted. Pete and his family had spent the years 1950-1951 in Germany. His father had been part of a Lutheran World Relief team resettling World War II refugees.

With that experience and his college major in German language, Pete enlisted in the Air Force, thinking that he would be stationed in Germany.

He was, and our daughter Lisa and I joined him. He worked at a military base, but we lived on the economy and I became familiar with the small shops which were common at that time.

Winter weather in Germany is often cold and damp and few homes ten years after the end of World War II had central heating, so one dressed oneself warmly for indoors and for outdoors. During our time there, I found some shops specializing in angora fiber products.

The German angora industry dates back almost 100 years, is strictly regulated, and produces a yarn spun mostly of angora and merino wool.

This yarn was, and is, knitted commercially into a variety of warm undergarments. These were, and are, expensive, but if the purchase was accompanied by a doctor's prescription for nonmedical relief from arthritic pain, the health service paid for it.

In 1958 our family moved back to the United States. We were now four; Mike had been born in Germany.

Considering what he should do next, Pete decided to study for a teacher's degree in German language.

Acquiring that, he found a teaching position here in the Blue Earth's schools. It was late summer in 1960 when we moved to Blue Earth.

Our third child, Conrad, had been born in Minneapolis, and Sarah, our fourth, was born here in Blue Earth in late October 1960. Hanns, our fifth child, was born in 1964. We were all busy in school, church and community, but in 1971 we again went to Germany.

Pete had applied for a Fulbright teacher exchange. He got it, and following a few months of discussion and arrangements we moved into the home of Dieter and Marley Wollenteit in Kassel, Germany. They and their four children moved into our home in Blue Earth. After a year, we were back in Blue Earth, and they were back at their home in Kassel.

While in Kassel, we had arranged for a student exchange: Lisa, with the son of a Kassel family.

Our bedroom space was limited, so we moved to a new location, a small acreage on the edge of Blue Earth. During the next few years, we remodeled and redecorated and hosted several other exchange students. We also made use of our space, adding livestock.

It wasn't until 1981 that I seriously considered, as an adult, raising angora rabbits. Quite by happenstance, I came across an exhibit by French angora owner Corinne Pearson at the Martin County fair. I visited her rabbitry and bought from her my first breeding pair.

Subsequently, I acquired new French angora breeding stock from rabbit owners in Iowa, Minnesota, South Dakota, and Alaska. Also helpful to me were the discussions I held with these owners.

I participated in only one rabbit show, but I take a rabbit and a spinning wheel to our county fair and other local venues and spin yarn with a rabbit on my lap. Demonstrating the process and talking about it helps to sell those hand spun, hand-knitted items.

For many years I've done art and craft shows, generally, 'juried' shows. A daughter, either Lisa or Sarah, usually accompanies me. We've always had rabbits and a spinning wheel with us.

I'm writing this as a handbook for those who may be interested in raising a herd of angoras and / or making use of their fiber. I like to manage every stage of the craft, from selection and breeding to production of wearables. I regularly do it all myself but also delegate to others. I view this traditional approach as similar to what I experienced as a child, growing up where one managed livestock from birth to the dinner table. I consider myself to be a craft person. To some, I may be 'the bunny lady' or even a rabbit farmer.

It is my hope that this book may be of use to anyone who approaches any of the aspects of rabbit farming. I've arranged the following chapters in what would be a sequential progression of my development of the craft, but I have attempted to make each chapter stand on its own. In this way, the reader can access any chapter out of sequence as their need arises.

My own experience has been anything but tackling each topic one at a time. Every new challenge arose in its own time over forty years, and often I experienced all at once the complexities of building out my herd, learning to house them, breeding them, keeping them happy and healthy and discovering all the things one can make with the wool.

I've included resources to assist the crafter and references to flesh out details where more are needed. I include techniques for harvesting the wool, processing the felt, making wearable items and fiber art novelties. Supplementing the appendices are online resources with drawings, photos and demonstration videos at the following link:

ACKNOWLEDGEMENTS

Kay Bogen, master knitter

Jane Leverenz, master knitter

Bob Bogen, Veterinarian

Lisa Lindberg

Mike Lindberg

Micah Lindberg

Sarah Lindberg Maass

Every member of the family

My supportive husband, Peter Lindberg

> (Once, Pete, a teacher, took bunnies to his middle school German classes. This was the banter as the kids left the classroom: ("Du hast lange Ohren." "Nein, DU has lange Ohren!")

Paul C Kuehner, my father, who gave me the angoras as a gift at the age of ten

All the shopkeepers I met during our time in Germany

Corrine Pearson – For my first breeding pair.

I'm grateful to my entire family for their help in this venture from the manufacture of rabbit coops to the transcription of the material that I've written. Mike, Lisa and Micah have been most involved. Lisa established the Acorn Studio in Amboy, which features my angora products - in addition to other handcrafted items, particularly caps, sweaters, etc. knitted by Jane Leverenz.

Other persons who've – how would I say – who've been involved in this venture are Bob Bogen, Veterinarian, and Kay Bogen, master knitter, and Jane Leverenz, also a master knitter. Our local community itself has been very helpful. I've done numerous demonstrations, spent time demonstrating my spinning at the local county fair, and I sell items at our craft shows that are put on in southern Minnesota. My thanks to those who have provided me with new breeding stock, persons from Minnesota, Iowa, Wisconsin, South Dakota and Alaska. And special thanks to the persons who wrote the book "Complete Angoras" Leslie Sampson and Sharon Kilfoyle. And the book "Rabbit Production". Those were my chief sources. But I've also subscribed to monthly magazines and brochures such as <u>House Rabbit Journal</u>, <u>Pacific Angora Fanciers - and fiber artists -</u> (PAFFA), <u>Angora Today</u> and <u>Rabbits Today</u>. My thanks to a long-distance friend Louise Lindley, from St Petersburg, Alaska, who has bought quite a lot of raw wool from me. She's an English teacher who is also a Spinner, and probably a knitter; she does shows as well. Granddaughter Mia Lindberg also helped with photos, demonstration videos and copy editing.

THE ANIMAL

Angora Breeds

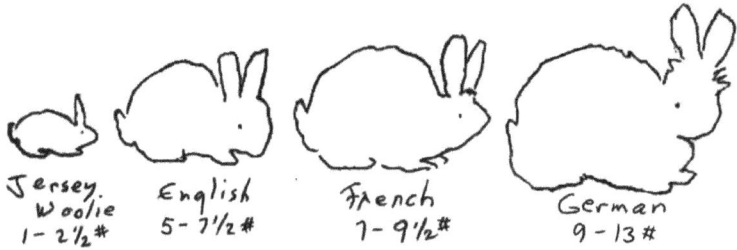

There are several breeds of angora rabbit. They range in size from the Jersey Wooly to the German.

These are the most common breeds; they are all long haired, but hair growth differs in structure, length and quantity.

I started with French angora, and that is the rabbit that I have continued to raise. In body structure they are similar to the New Zealand White rabbit, and they are considered a dual-purpose animal, used for both meat and wool. The wool of the French angora is somewhat coarser than that of the English, and develops good length. It does not mat as easily as the English. It generally has more guard hairs, is more highly pigmented, and works out in knitted garments. This I especially like in headgear, with its "halo" effect.

Since all of my animals are in outdoor quarters, for me, the French angora makes the most sense. I do most of the hair removal by plucking; and after that loose coat is removed, there are still two shorter coats left for warmth. Plucking has long been the usual form of harvesting French angora wool. Over the generations, this has probably determined the hair growth pattern. The French rabbit hair growth is in three layers. The outer layer is plucked when it gets loose. The other two layers provide continued warmth, ideal for outdoor living in a cold climate.

Every two or three months, the second layer will become the outer layer and loosen, and will need to be removed. I pluck each animal about five or six times a year. That is when I groom them, too. They generally don't need more than a quick brushing and a combing to prepare for each plucking. In a year's time, a good 'wooler' may provide me with a pound of wool.

Most English coats are finer and require more grooming because they generally mat more easily. There are those rabbit fanciers who groom weekly.

The German hair structure is different from the French; It does not shed, and needs to be clipped or shorn periodically, usually every three months. I have not had the German breed. I understand that their genome includes a gene that inhibits felting.

The Jersey Wooly may have enough hair in a year's time for a headband or a soft addition to a wool yarn.

Generally, all of the larger angora breeds are considered to be gentle and easy to work with. The Jersey Wooly has a reputation for a bad attitude. I haven't had any Woolies, so I can't verify that, but there are clubs of enthusiastic Jersey Wooly owners who may know otherwise.

Angora History

According to legend, long-haired rabbits, cats, sheep and goats were originally developed in Ankara, Turkey. Information about them after that is scarce, but the modern wool industry is supposed to have started in France in the later 1700s.

During the French Revolution, angora rabbits had been pets of the aristocracy, and when their owners were done away with, they were too. However – some of these pets were spirited away by the commoners, who started to raise them in their backyards. I haven't been able to find much information on further development but at a show in Albert Lea, MN, a visitor stopped by my booth and looked at some felted insoles, and remarked, "my grandmother used to make something like these; she lived in Poland".

Now, angora fiber is widely used in Europe, primarily for its warmth. In Germany, what we all call the German angora has been standardized from the early 1900s and is an important part of the commercial undergarment industry. The angora is blended together with other fibers – notably, merino wool and Viscose for stability and washability. These items are exceptional for their warmth, softness, and durability.

German health insurance plans will pay for these items if they are prescribed for therapeutic use.

Some other nations have their own "national" angora. What the genetics are I don't know. I suspect that they are of French or German stock.

HOW DO ANGORA AND LAMBSWOOL COMPARE?

1. If a person has an allergy to wool, he/she may not be allergic to angora. The reverse may also be true.

2. Wool varies more with regard to softness and coarseness (correlating hair shaft width, measured in microns).

3. Wool is very sensitive to water temperature changes when washing it. Angora is not.

4. Wool fibers have barbs on them which, together with the sensitivity to temperature changes, make felting easier and faster. Angora has small scales on its fibers, which do not seem to do much to help the felting process.

5. Angora is very lightweight. Except for the outer guard hair, angora has a smaller hair shaft width than the finer wools. It is also a "hollow fiber" - much like water reeds - with many small spaces within the fiber shaft.

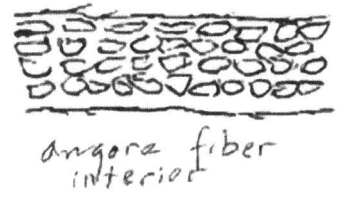

angora fiber interior

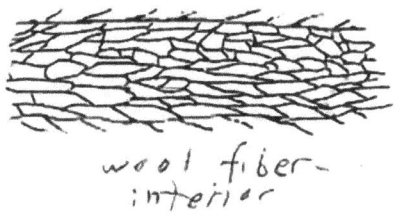

wool fiber interior

6. Lambswool is a dense fiber all the way through. It is, consequently, heavier. This difference is very noticeable when you wash the finished items. Angora will float on the water for hours if undisturbed. Wool sinks.

7. Because of the number of fibers and their "hollow" structure, angora is much warmer than lambswool. It's surprising when one first experiences it. Angora is - by weight - seven to eight times warmer than wool. One would have to wear three or four pairs of lambswool mittens to equal the mount of insulative quality of one pair of angora mittens.

8. I hear frequent complaints about wool being "scratchy". Not so, angora. However, in a garment with a lot of angora guard hair, there could be complaints.

9. Angora is a rather unpredictable fiber - it can be hard to work with! I think that it's no wonder that it's not a popular commercial addition to our American garments. However, it *is* popular as an attractive and warm addition to sweaters and other clothing items. Otherwise, here in the U.S., it seems, it is mostly used as decoration.

10. Angora blends well with other fine fibers such as alpaca, silk, kid mohair, tencel and the finer lambswools such as merino and romney. The addition of these and other fibers to the angora can add interest – and keep the garment from being too warm for indoor wear.

BUILDING YOUR HERD

Choosing your Stock

Whether you want one or two angoras as pets or have the intention of setting up a rabbitry you want to make sure you have good stock. In choosing a bunny, you want one with bright eyes, a curious nature, a compact body, and a dry nose. You don't want a respiratory problem! You want no excrement on the underside of the body, and you want free flowing fiber - no mats - no greasy feel to the skin, as this could be evidence of hair mites. These can be responsible for matting, particularly in the hindquarters.

Gender is considered in choosing livestock, and some will consider it in choosing a pet. Attitude can differ by gender: males are considered by some owners to be "more interesting" -perhaps because their reproductive drive – testosterone - promotes a greater level of, shall we say, "social outreach". This will be less pronounced if the buck is neutered.

In a young rabbit, distinguishing males from females can be confusing. I have goofed a number of times! In a male, the testicles descend around 3½ to 4 months of age, and the skin on either side of the penis is without hair. The female has hair on both sides of her vagina, which is a longish slit.

If you are looking for a pet or a 4H project, you need to do some research. Will your rabbit need a pedigree? Does your animal need to conform to the ARBA (American rabbit breeders' association) standard? Check this out. Even the color of the toenails is important.

Most angoras make good pets. They are bred to be handled. Most of them are gentle and compliant. Those that are not don't go to shows with me.

If it's a pet you want, it's not necessary to have pedigree papers, but if you plan to show your animal, you do want those papers. These papers trace the rabbit's genealogy - that is ancestry, back 3 generations, and they do not necessarily note color, weight, or wool production. If your bunny is pedigreed, you will probably pay more for him or her, and you need to buy only from a rabbit breeder who can provide a record of the pedigree.

Getting an animal registered is another matter. It must have a pedigree, be examined by a licensed ARBA registrar, and conform to the ARBA standard of perfection for that breed. If interested, contact a registrar or take the rabbit to an ARBA sanctioned show.

You also want to make sure that your first breeding pair came from different bloodlines because you want to avoid the health problems which may arise from the inbreeding of recessive genes.

It's a good idea to actually see the rabbits you are buying. Is the rabbitry relatively clean and organized? Does the owner seem to enjoy working with the rabbits? Look around at the rabbits themselves. Are there any runny noses or sneezing? These are an indication of respiratory problems which you want to avoid.

If you are planning to buy one or more angoras, bear in mind that those cute little bunnies grow into some rather large rabbits. The German and Giants reach about 12 or 13 pounds, the French 9 or 10, the English 6 or 7, and the Jersey Wooly about 2 pounds. Most of my angoras - all French - are quite mellow, and are cooperative when I groom and pluck them.

Planning ahead

Plan ahead before you buy your rabbits! Think about where you will house the animals. In what kind of coop or structure will you keep them? Where will you keep the feed? How will you provide for water? For cleaning? Rabbits, as vegans, produce lots of droppings (if they are healthy). Prepare your rabbits' living quarters before you bring your bunnies home. Refer to the section on housing and the appendix for housing suppliers, or ask any handyman in your family for some help.

Genetics

There always seems to be controversy regarding the role of genetics vs environment. The accepted combination is 50/50 - for all of us - humans, cows, pigs, dogs, cats, whooping cranes, rabbits. Bodies are made up of trillions of cells which contain the building blocks of the animal itself or of the next generation.

Each cell contains a nucleus, which is the command center of the cell. This nucleus contains the chromosomes which contain the DNA and the RNA, the templates of growth and development or the templates of reproduction. All but one of these cells is called a somatic cell. (TEMPLETON 1982, 217) These somatic cells direct the growth of the animal. That one unique cell contains a sex - related chromosome, and is responsible for the next generation.

Each species contains a specific number of chromosomes in the nuclei. Human cells contain 46, rabbits 44. Chromosome numbers may be expressed in pairs, signaling the inheritance of two individuals. The one unique chromosome, the sex chromosome, is only half of the total number in each individual. In rabbits, this is 22. In the process of fertilization, the male sperm cell, containing either an X or a Y chromosome, penetrates the female ovum, or egg, which contains only an X chromosome.

The actual union of male and female sex cells happens a few hours after breeding, and the implantation of the zygote (the fertilized egg) some hours later.

Upon fertilization, similar numbers of chromosome pairs unite, restoring the number of chromosomes in each cell to 44.

Since chromosomes are inherited in pairs, half of these come from the buck and half from the dam (doe). These chromosomes contain the genes (DNA) of each individual.

Variations of the DNA (alleles) at certain locations on each chromosome of a pair encode for the animal's resulting hair color, hair length, color density, color pattern, and many other traits. The way each trait is expressed in the animal (phenotype) depends on the combined alleles for that trait from both buck and dam.

Alleles can be recessive or dominant; that is, for a recessive gene, both buck and dam need to contribute the same recessive allele for that corresponding trait to be expressed in the offspring. Conversely, a gene will express if either one or both contributed alleles are dominant for that trait.

Dominant genes are usually represented by a capitalized letter, while recessive are lower case. Recognized paired combinations and their resulting coat characteristics include:

Normal / Angora	LL, ll, Ll, lL	Results in angora hair only for ll pair, otherwise normal hair.
Color Density	BB, bb, Bb, bB	Results in chocolate color only for bb pair, otherwise black hair. B also produces an agouti (see below) coat.
Agouti	AA, aa, Aa, aA	Results in "wild" color distribution for the dominant gene A and Tan color for the recessive a^t
Color Series	CC or Cc	Will result in full color, likely the agouti (wild) color. The cc combination results in an albino color.
Dilute	D	Results in higher density "more solid" coat color, d results in more dilute color
Extension	E	Encodes for normal extension of dark color, as controlled by allele B. Lower case e will not.

A lower case "l" "long hair" allele will result in an angora offspring, both buck and dam each need to contribute a recessive allele. An angora offspring will not result if a "dominant" (L) type variant is contributed by either buck or dam.

Since recessive traits such as coat color depend partly on recessive genes, when you are choosing your animals for breeding, you want to think of the next generation. The phenotype (the observed coat color) is quite obvious, but not always a trustworthy indication of genotype (the genes). There is a good example to map the probabilities of producing an angora offspring based on proportions of the angora trait dominant and recessive L gene (SAMPSON 1992, 56) as well as a more detailed mapping of coat colors for various allele combinations (SAMPSON 1992, 60).

Studying the genotype of each animal may be helpful here (the pedigree papers should be helpful). A bit of research (check ARBA) should also be considered.

If you are convinced that you have a desirable breeding pair, your chief concern with your wool-bearing angoras will probably be color.

When considering the coat color, the dominant gene comes from the original wild rabbit, which has the agouti hair pattern. This is a banded tan with black guard hair.

The agouti is also distinguished by light tan on the breast and undersides and light tan around the eyes.

This dominant gene is denoted in the literature by a capital "E". It can also be a recessive gene, influencing other genes which are expressed as a small e. (TEMPLETON 1982, 224)

Black is also a dominant gene, expressed as a capital "B". However, each of these dominant genes may have alleles, that is, recessive genes that may influence the present generation or the next. There is also a dominant C gene but it is a fixed combination of the recessive "cc" (One recessive from each animal).

In accepted notation, the "ll" combination determines the recessive long hair characteristic of the angora bunny. The remaining combinations, in the following examples

White: llcc	->	recessive Albino
Black: llaa	->	recessive Agouti
Blue: llaadd	->	recessive Agouti: and recessive Black
Fawn: llee	->	recessive genes from the Agouti pattern.

The "L" in the genome is for normal hair structure; the "l" is for the angora.

To summarize, two recessives (one from each parent) will result in a full color coat (but may be influenced by other genes). A dominant gene will mask (or hide) a recessive gene.

A few definitions:

Alleles	-	Two or more genes at a locus.
Chromosome	-	The largest unit of inheritance found in the nucleus. It's made of DNA and RNA and inherited in pairs.
Diploid	-	A complete set of paired chromosomes.
Gametogenesis	-	Formation of sex cells in the testes and the ovaries.
Gametes	-	Sex cells.
Gene	-	The basic unit of inheritance.
Haploid	-	A sex cell that contains only one member from each chromosome pair. Upon fertilization, similar members of chromosome pairs unite (22 male + 22 female) = 44, the whole, or Diploid number.
Homozygote	-	Identical alleles at a specific locus: The albino "cc" is an example.
Heterozygote	-	A mix of genes. Mating a heterozygous rabbit to an albino will result in 50% albino (cc) and 50% colored.
Locus	-	A specific region on the chromosome where a particular gene is found.
Meiosis	-	The process of cell division that results in the formation of sex cells.
Mitosis	-	The form of division in somatic cells. The cell divides, producing two identical daughter cells.

Mutation	-	A spontaneous change in the structure of a gene. The result is a sudden, heritable change in the offspring. This is very rare. Most often such occurrences are two rare recessive genes getting together. Most actual mutations are generally lethal. However, albinism was the result of such a mutation centuries ago and was desirable, because such pelts could be dyed.
Nucleus	-	A cellular organelle found in all body cells.
Zygotes	-	Fertilized ova or egg.

BREEDING

When you breed your rabbits, you are thinking about perpetuating the best qualities in both male and female. Keep in mind that both animals possess both dominant and recessive genes.

Start your herd by buying from two separate bloodlines. Looking at your pedigree papers, you may see that the grandparents or great-grandparents were unrelated with the following generation. You'll probably see something called "linebreeding" (SAMPSON 1992, 52). This is breeding two related animals together, such as grandfather to granddaughter or nephew to aunt. This system is one you may wish to continue until you experience the arrival of the evidence of some unwanted recessive genes, such as those that are responsible for undescended testicles or Wolf teeth.

With inbreeding you mate closely related animals such as father - daughter, sister - brother. This system heightens the chances that those undesirable recessive genes will get together and exhibit themselves in the new generation. This system should be managed so that you can get rid of those recessive genes and you need to be ready to cull these animals when they show up.

Some definitions.

Outcrossing	-	Breeding two unrelated animals of the same breed.
Inbreeding	-	Breeding two closely related animals such as mother and son, father - daughter, brother-sister.
Linebreeding	-	Breeding two more distantly related individuals.
Outbreeding	-	The same as outcrossing.
Crossbreeding	-	Breeding two animals from different breeds such as angora/Rex or angora/New Zealand. This is probably the method by which most colored angoras arrived on the scene but we can't discount the influence of that wild agouti gene. If you should want to try this, it will take several generations to get a more or less stable angora inheritance.

Mating

Rabbits breed year – round, but here, with a cold climate and my rabbits out of doors, I prefer not to breed from October – March.

Before breeding the doe, pluck or clip her hair. The long hair could wind around babies' legs and cut off circulation. To breed the doe, put her in with the buck. You may put the buck in with the doe, but that is her space and she may give him a hard time. When you put the doe in with the buck, he will likely not waste any time. After mating happens, he will flop over on his side from exhaustion and you can assume that the doe has been bred. He will get up right away.

If he keeps mounting her, take her out. Otherwise, you may want them to continue to enjoy their companionship for a while. When you return the doe to her coop, consider: could a newborn crawl through the screen? If the spacing is about an inch, it's too wide. In this case, attach about 6" of hardware cloth half-inch screen around the bottom sides of the coop.

Gestation

Breeding itself results, hopefully, in fertilization. Gestation for a rabbit is about thirty days, and the litter sizes may vary from two to thirteen.

If you want to find out whether or not the doe's breeding was successful, the easiest way to determine this is to put the doe in with a buck, (either the same one or another) a few days after breeding. If the buck is not interested in her, she is probably pregnant. Another way to check is to palpate the doe's belly about ten days after breeding. Place the doe on a flat surface. Hold her in place with one hand and slide the other hand under her belly, and carefully feel for some marble-sized lumps. These would be the developing fetuses.

Delayed Kindling

Once in a long while I have a doe who I think is at term: I can see the babies, feel the babies, she may have milk. Her vulva is dark pink and enlarged. If I count twenty-eight to thirty-five days and nothing has happened, I just let the doe reabsorb those babies and decide to not breed her again.

From my further reading, this could be a genetic problem called uterine inertia. This is when the uterine horns lack the ability to contract and move the young into birthing position. Similar in appearance to this may be a condition in which the doe does not have enough energy to deliver babies. Administering orally one CC of corn syrup or molasses every four hours may help this.

The problem could also be a pregnancy toxemia. This can possibly be helped by giving a calcium supplement: One half cup of fresh broccoli daily for a week before kindling. It this helps, continue the broccoli for a few days after the kits are born.

False Pregnancy

With rabbits, there is no seasonal or hormonal readiness for mating. In the Spring, however, an un-mated female may do some frenzied nest building. When you see hay or hair in her mouth, her hair has probably loosened. If you want to pluck her, do so, because she will build that nest. Plucking her may confuse her and stop her current obsession. If the nest is completed and you find hair in the nest or outside of it, it may be possible for you to salvage some of the fiber. Don't bother if there is a lot of hay mixed in with it, but if I find it in sausage shapes it's probably fairly clean. Those are probably quite short, but after cleaning out the bits of debris, I use it for felt.

Kindling

A week before kindling, that is giving birth, place a nest box of about one square foot size in the doe's coop. In my outdoor coops with nest boxes the width of the coop, I put this smaller cardboard box with about 6" high sides in a corner. Put absorbent material in the bottom of this box. Newspaper is good but disposable diapers absorb best. Put some straw or hay in the box on top of that.

Provide more straw and hay for the doe. Again, make sure that the wire spacing around the bottom of the coop sides is close enough (½ inch) so that no babies can crawl through.

Sometimes the doe will start nesting activity a week or two after breeding. You may want to check her status at this point and put her back in with the buck. If he is not interested, put her back in her coop. Normally, the doe will wait until a couple of days before kindling to build her nest, but not always. That can be very frustrating!

When she is serious about preparing for those babies, she will gather straw and/or hay in her mouth and make a nest, hopefully in the box you have prepared. If you regularly put fresh forage in her coop, she may use some of it to line her nest. Take it out.

After she has prepared her nest, she starts pulling her hair from her breast and nipple area - and possibly sides. Sometimes she will pull so much hair that she ends up looking like she has a Mohawk! - If the amount of wool seems excessive, remove part of it, bag it, and put her name or number on it in case you need it later on... Check the length of that hair, too; clip it into 1" lengths or less so that babies won't get tangled in it.

Leave her alone now. She probably will have the babies at night, but not always. Check every few hours. When she has had her litter, she will have fed and cleaned each kit in turn, and covered them all with a cloud of hair. If that cloud moves a bit, you'll know the kits are there.

The doe is usually very protective, so don't bother her more than is necessary, but in a few hours you'll want to check to make sure that all is well. You may need to isolate the mother while you inspect; but if you take her out of the coop, when you return her, she may be very upset and possibly stomp on those babies.

After the doe gives birth she eats the placenta, and once in a while she ends up eating parts of the newborn - which might possibly be stillborn or deformed. Remove any dead baby bunnies, and any other birthing tissue.

Check the babies every day when you feed the mother. For a week or two, she will stimulate urination in the kits, so the nest will remain dry. When the babies begin to urinate without mom's stimulation, the nest material will need to be changed.

One time I left a litter in with the mother too long and one of those precocious young bucks of previous litter bred her right after she had had a new litter. Sloppy management, that! Upset with myself, I took the older bunnies out of the coop and separated males from females. The mother delivered that new litter thirty days later, all healthy. So, a doe could bear young every thirty days - give or take a couple of days - but that's not a good idea for either the mother or the babies. Three to five litters a year gives them more time to recuperate and the young to become independent of mom.

Growth and Development

The mother will feed her babies once or twice a day. Check them when you feed her. As her babies grow, she will eat increasing amounts of feed. Make sure she has plenty of clean water, and if she is accustomed to having treats, continue giving them to her.

Reverting to her wild ancestry, the mother spends very little time in the nest with her young. They will nurse very quickly - in ten minutes or less. Once in a while a baby will hang on to her as the mother leaves the nest, and it may be dropped on the cage floor. She will not return the baby to the nest, so you need to be aware of that.

That's the main reason for the smaller screen. It surprised me when one day I was pitching hay in the barn loft and saw a desperate mother mouse carrying a marble sized ball to another location. She made repeat runs. I guess mouse nests are better hidden than rabbit nests. In the wild, the mother rabbit cannot risk exposing the rest of her litter in the nest.

At about ten days of age the babies' eyes start opening, and at that point they become quite jumpy for two or three days. They are rather like popcorn popping when you inspect them. They may jump so high that they may jump right out of the nest box. I had one do that, and didn't find it until two or three days later - curled up at the base of a tree. He was still alive - and very hungry!

Three weeks after birth, the kits will start leaving the nest box. Once they start that, lower the sides of the box so that the kits are able to move freely about on their own. Provide additional water, hay and feed for the mother so that the kits have something to start nibbling on.

Also, about this time or a bit earlier, the babies no longer need mom's milk and may be moved to new quarters. You could wait a week or two before taking mom out - but if she doesn't allow any to move, it's time for her to be moved out. Put males in one coop, and females in another.

You most likely know who is what, but it's very easy to identify them incorrectly. So, check again. The male penis looks like a short hollow stem, and there is no hair growing up close to it. This is where the testicles will descend at about 3½ to 4 months of age.

Make sure that there is plenty of water and hay. As for pellets and grain, the amount should be what the kits will readily eat. The demand for this feed will increase as the bunnies grow. If you were feeding the mother and her young some fresh treats, continue this, but limit it. Diarrhea can result from too much.

At about eight to ten weeks, I give the kits their first haircut. Brush and comb the coat. With a small, sharp scissors, clip close to the skin (Be careful, it's very tender.) If there are mats, make sure that you get all of the matted fiber removed. With a metal brush and comb, clean out any debris and tangles. Get the underside as well as the back.

The junior's hair is long enough at five months of age for the second hair removal. You may try doing a little plucking at this time, but clipping is easier for the bunnies whose skin is still quite sensitive. By this time, you probably also had to separate the males from each other because they will start fighting each other. You have also checked the females, making sure there is not a buck among them.

From this fiber I make a lightweight felt that I use for example, for gnome jackets and trousers - things that don't get hard use.

Again, brush and comb, and remove any mats. Pluck whatever is loose if you want to pluck - but all of the hair should again be removed. Use your little sharp scissors and get as close to the skin as you can. Any old residual fibers will combine with the new fiber and create a new mat. (If you should happen to cut the skin, it will quickly heal - but putting a bit of antibiotic on the cut is a good idea). Finish by making sure that all of the hair is clipped, and brush and comb again. After you are done, the rabbits will groom themselves again.

If you haven't already done it, this is a good time to tattoo the bunnies' ears. More on that subject is in the upcoming section on tatooing.

Foster Care

When you breed, it can be advantageous to breed two does at the same time. That way, if one of the mothers has too few babies - or too many - the moms can share. Mark the fostered babies' ears with permanent marker so that your pedigree papers have accurate information. There can be a week or two difference in the ages of the kits, but not much more. If a doe dies and leaves a litter motherless, you can try to add the babies to an older litter, but it may or may not work. Sometimes it does.

If you need to provide other formula for babies, rabbit formula is probably difficult to find. Rat milk is the one milk that is close - high in protein and fat. Probably, goat's milk is better than cow's milk. Feed with a doll bottle or an eyedropper, and as the babies grow, add some oat flour or oat milk. No lumps!

The mother normally nurses her young only once or twice a day, but if you are giving supplement, do it somewhat more often.

When you feed these newborn, you need to take over the mother's job of stimulating urination. Wet a finger and stroke the little urethra or penis until the baby urinates. You'll need to do this until you notice in a week or two that the nest is getting wet. It's probably best to do this before feeding.

Litter Size

Litters vary in size – I think that six kits is an optimal number but they can vary in number from two to thirteen. In my experience, the litter of thirteen all grew up strong and healthy. A litter of two or three may be a problem. The mother may have more milk than the kits can eat and she may develop mastitis (SAMPSON 1992, 71). If she develops a fever and her teats become red and swollen, cut back on her feed – and you may want to administer penicillin. Small litter size isn't always a factor in mastitis.

Some rabbit breeders cull kits at birth, making decisions that fit their goals.

Identification - Tattooing

If you are building a herd, you will need to buy tattoo equipment. Tattooing not only is necessary if you go to shows or sell your animals, but it helps to keep your records in order. It's a good idea to record these chronologically as you increase your herd.

All tattoo methods puncture the skin, and tattoo ink – or India Ink – is rubbed into the perforations. All are unpleasant for the rabbit. Electric tattoo machines vibrate and work more gradually to break the skin but they are much more expensive. A simple punch, like a pair of pliers, has one jaw to hold the number and letter digits and another with a rubber pad, which presses the tattoo into the ear.

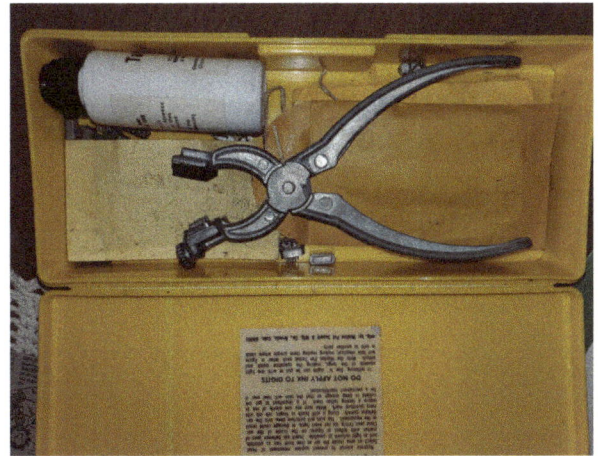

With the punch, you are limited as to the number of digits – probably five. You need a tattoo that at least shows birthdate and animal number. Choose these and place these in your punch, secure them with the screws at the top of that jaw. Do not put ink on the digits.

Have ready – your tattoo tool with appropriate digits, alcohol and swabs, the tattoo ink, with the application roller.

If you need to restrain your bunny for this procedure, I find that wrapping him or her in a towel on my lap with just the head and ears showing is the easiest for both of us. For this identification, you use the left ear. The right ear is saved for a registration number if you choose to do that.

Look carefully at the ear in the light and find a bare area that avoids the two veins that surround that area. You may want to hold an ice cube to the area to deaden it a bit. Rub the inside of that left ear with alcohol and place the padded jaw of the tool on the outside of that bare spot. Now carefully place the jaw with digits against the inside of the ear and press. There may be screaming – hopefully not too much blood. Remove the pliers and rub tattoo ink or India Ink into the perforations with your finger or the ink roller. Be thorough – use enough to fill the tiny holes.

When done, wipe off the excess ink with a dry swab. The ear will heal in a couple of days.

I bought a tattoo set with plastic digits and it was less expensive, but after a while some of the plastic digits bent at the tips. It may be worth it for you to buy the set with metal digits.

Neutering

An important disclaimer!

Not everyone is likely to feel comfortable with the following description of the neutering process. I am not a veterinarian, and this passage is written only to describe my own experience. Although some parts of the process described here have been used on many kinds of livestock over the years, I do not claim any authority in the subject and accept no responsibility for your use or your decision to use techniques presented here, or for any resulting damages, illness or injury based on any person using this material. Always consult a professional if you need help.

Adult male angoras need to be housed individually. If they are, possibly you'll find that you will get more wool from them than from the adult females. Those does, whether they are really having babies or are just imagining that they are, can waste quite a lot of wool (though it makes good compost).

My goal from the start was to raise the rabbits in colonies. I learned early that each rabbit has his or her own personality and that arranging them in companionable groups is tricky. Furthermore, those males cannot be grouped together. So - how was I to fix that?

Neutering was the answer: A neutered male will generally coexist peaceably with females or other neutered males.

How should this be done? I couldn't find any literature that would enable me to do this procedure by myself. A son-in-law who had castrated piglets volunteered to do a mass castration for me. I had fourteen young bucks sitting on chairs around my kitchen table, and my son-in-law got to work.

All seemed to go well but when I checked those rabbits in the morning five had died - probably from internal bleeding. Was I upset? YES. That was not a good plan. Piglets most likely have tougher tissues than rabbits.

Next, quite a while later, I set up an appointment with my veterinarian to neuter five young bucks. Of the five, one was cryptorchid which would have required invasive surgery. One (my favorite) received the minimum amount of anesthetic and promptly died. The 3rd buck received the maximum dose of anesthetic and didn't go under. The procedure went well for the last two.

So - that didn't go as I had hoped.

Then I remembered that we had neutered new lambs by "banding them" using a tool called an "elastrator". We stretched a small but heavy rubber band over each testicle. Following that, the lamb lay down for an hour or two, but soon he was up - and doing well. In a few days, the testicles dried up and fell off.

This I decided would probably work for rabbits. With rabbits, however, the testicles don't descend until the animal is three or four months old and I wait to do this until the testicles are almost adult size. Wait until the bunny is six months old. I don't neuter any rabbits this way if they are over a year old; the skin is heavier then and I am not sure that this procedure can keep blood from the testicles. Probably, surgical castration is then your best bet.

Young bucks awaiting their turn

The neutering Procedure that I use:

In my Arsenal:

1.   Several small rubber bands, white or natural color

2.   A small dish with alcohol to soak the rubber bands in

3.   Cotton balls

4.   Dental floss

5.   A towel

6.   Small sharp scissors

This is the procedure itself:

1.   Place your bunny on a towel on your lap.

2.   Turn him over on his back and massage his tummy. (This kind of hypnotizes him)

3. Using your little scissors, remove all of the hair around the testicles. You don't want any hair under the rubber band.

4. He is positioned with his back legs near your knees.

5. Continue to massage his tummy. Decide which testicle you are going to do first. If it disappears inside his body, stroke that area or just wait a while until it pops out.

6. Take a cotton ball soaked in the alcohol and swab the testicle and surrounding area.

7. Remove a rubber band from the alcohol and hold it open with two or three fingers.

8. With the other hand, press down on the place where the testicle enters the abdomen to keep it from slipping back. QUICKLY put the expanded rubber band all the way down to the abdomen. Twist it around the testicle three or four times. Get it as tight as you can. (You are going to get some resistance.) Wait a bit.

9. Measure off about eight inches of dental floss, and tie that, too, around the testicle. This you can pull really tight. No blood should get through.

10. Let your bunny rest a bit, massage his tummy and do the second testicle.

11. Swab the area again with alcohol.

Generally, by the day after, you will see both testicles shrinking. Eventually - maybe in five days - they will dry up and fall off.

I'm sure that over the years I've neutered around 100 bucks. I've never lost a rabbit doing the neutering this way, but I neuter one at a time and I keep him in a cage nearby so that I can check on him. He will feel odd for a while but then he will resume his normal behavior.

What follows is a kind of diary that I kept after one procedure. Why I documented it, I don't know. I didn't expect there to be a problem, but it did get worrisome. Early on day four, I injected subcutaneously one-half CC of penicillin.

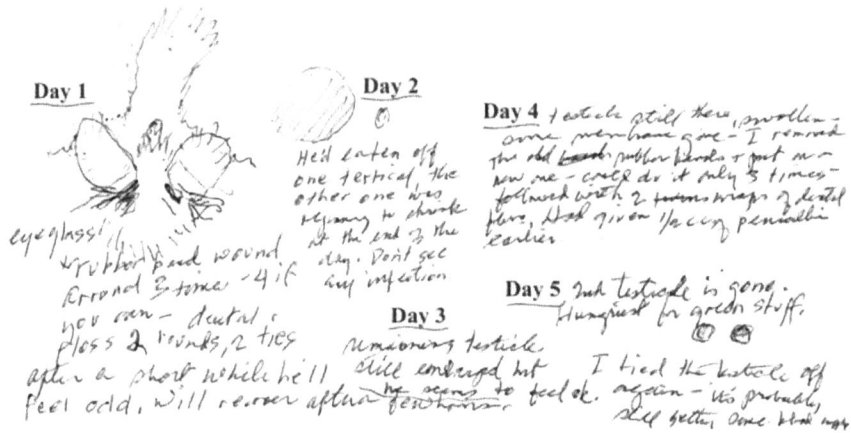

An excerpt from my notes of the procedure

When the testicles have dried up and/or fallen off, return the bunny to his pen, and keep him there for at least a week to make sure that there is no more semen available. (I put a neutered buck in with a doe five days after neutering, and babies resulted.)

I find that a neutered buck/doe combination is usually the most harmonious…but harmony doesn't always happen right away.

HOUSING

Most rabbit breeders who raise rabbits commercially have their animals housed inside, often in buildings that can be heated, having electricity and running water.

Adult rabbits are housed separately in wire coops or cages, the largest, 30 by 36 or 36 by 30 inches.

Those are often provided with nesting areas, often a drop nest arrangement. Juniors are sometimes housed together until the buck is sexually mature, as early as three months! Coops are often suspended from the ceiling and sometimes an automatic watering system is in place. Food containers are attached to the coop screen.

With angoras, a wire hay holder is often also attached to the screen.

Trudging through snow in the Winter, I think of how nice it would be if my animals were inside - but with them in outside coops I never smell ammonia - more common in enclosed spaces, especially with concrete floors.

As long as we've had school age kids, we've had one or two pet rabbits. They were all short haired and lived in outside coops or hutches - whatever we could find or put together.

When I bought my first trio of angoras, they too were housed in outdoor coops, mostly donated. Why it happened, I don't know, because the coops seemed secure, but a couple of large roaming dogs upset the coops and killed some of the rabbits. Their owner had insurance and compensated me for my loss.

The payment was enough for me to buy posts and six-foot-high fencing for my "rabbit yard". Having done quite a bit of reading about raising animals "naturally", I divided the area into two spaces - one for bucks and one for does. That did not work. The bucks fought, and the does established cliques. My next experiment, and one that evolved over several years, was to create large pens with hog grating for flooring and sturdy fencing for separating pens. In these pens, I used a couple of types of housing.

One type was two halves of a fifty-gallon pickled onion barrel salvaged from our local canning factory. I had several of these. For each half I put in wood flooring and cut 4 inches long 4 x 4 blocks and nailed them under the floor. That keeps the coop off the ground. Cut a door in each of the shelters.

The other model was a small "A frame" that I made, 16" by 16" for the floor set on two-by-fours about 26" long. Two 16" by 16" pieces for the A frame roof and a triangular or rectangular piece to form the back. I nailed this assembly to the floor and added a 16" by 6" wide board to the two-by-four extensions for a "porch".

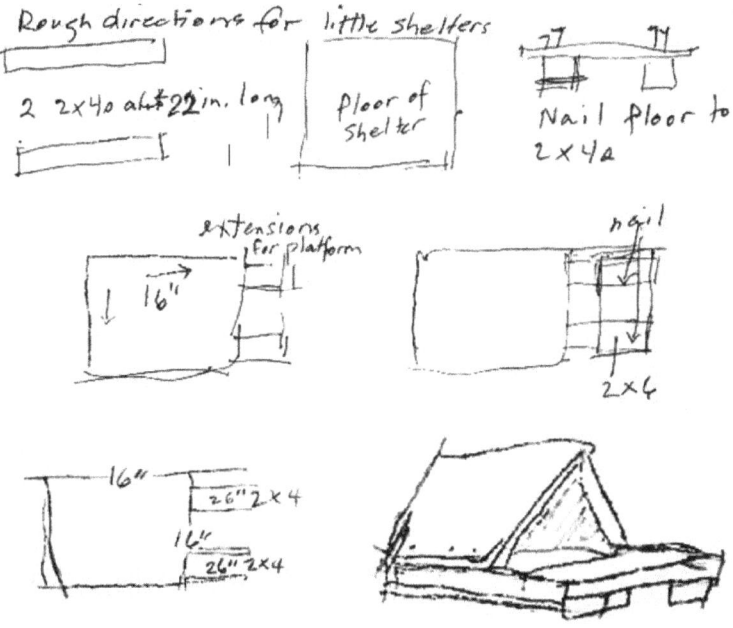

These little shelters were satisfactory for a long time. Even when there was a lot of winter snow, the rabbits would keep the entrances open. If it was wet, there was room enough in the shelters for a feed dish and some hay. Snow provided water.

My rabbit coops are in a well shaded area on a southern slope and there is generally a welcome breeze that helps them manage the heat.

Making the Housing Predator–proof

RHYMES WITH ORANGE HILARY PRICE

THE BIG NIGHT

Can you be ready for a chase at six thirty?

WILL YOU SWALLOW IT? I'M PROPOSING TO MY GIRLFRIEND AT DINNER AND WANT TO HIDE IT IN THE FOOD.

Cartoon graphic reprinted with permission of:
Rhymes With Orange © 2020 RWO Studios, Distributed by King Features Syndicate, Inc.

The downside of these open-top pens was the possibility of predators. We live in the curve of the Blue Earth River. At one time, trapping for mink, particularly, was done there. Pelts are not as valuable as they once were, but the mink are still around. Once in a long while I'd find one of my dead rabbits with a bite between the ears or a chewed section under the tail. For quite a while I wondered what beastie had done this… until one day I saw the legs of one of my chickens extending from the small door of the chicken house.

That was hardly normal, so I checked. In the corner of the coop was a cowering mink. A cat was chewing on his recent kill, so my husband shot the mink.

Now I knew what was killing my rabbits, so we put up 36" chicken wire all around the rabbit yard periphery and a strand of electric wire 20" from the ground. This worked well as long as the fence didn't short out - or I forgot to close the gate!

Yet another unwelcome visitor to my rabbit yard was a great horned owl. Over the space of two or three days, six rabbits were decapitated. Adults are probably too heavy for an owl to carry the entire animal, so it took the head and whatever came with it - six times! Seeing bird droppings at the base of one of those fence posts, I loosely tacked some sturdy 1" by 1" screen material to each post top. Whether or not I was correct in thinking that the owl had to sit to survey the territory before making his attack, I don't know, but I didn't lose any more rabbits to owls.

Not very long ago, as I approached the rabbit yard, a bald eagle flew up from inside the yard. The day before, one of my rabbits had escaped his pen. I never located him, so I suppose he was food for nestlings.

Now my rabbits are in eight-foot-long coops so they get some exercise. All are constructed from two by twos and two by fours, hardware cloth and lumber suitable for nest boxes and openings. Some roofing is optional.

Following my directions, a friend built these coops for me. See the figure.

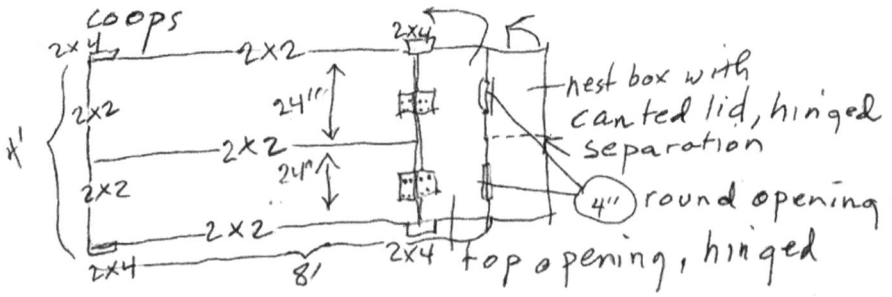

The sides are 18" high and the coop floor is about 18" from the ground. My single 8' long coops have canted roofs, are wood on one 8 ft side and service doors on the side near the nest box and at the end. That end door is really useful for cleaning.

I attached rings of wire to the side screen for water and obtained 303 size cans from the local Green Giant canning factory. The cans are easy to replace during the winter. I use crocks for feed. Rabbits dump lighter weight containers.

These new coops I have had for three or four years and I see that the hardware cloth is beginning to tear away from the connection to the 8' two by twos. If you can find heavier wire at least ½" by 1" gauge, do so. Don't double the hardware cloth. Droppings will get stuck.

More two-by-two cross pieces under the hardware cloth will help. Also, unless you include the nest box as part of the 8' length, you need to provide extra bracing for the nest box. Otherwise, it will pull away from the coop. Now I cannot add bracing to the 8' run. I put in lengths of board wide enough to reach both screen sides. I suppose those could be nailed on to the two-by-twos. The rabbits really enjoy that solid flooring.

Yet, over the years I've put together quite a few cages, all wire and for temporary use. Members of my family helped me with the building of coops or hutches. One such coop was all metal except for the roof and it was to last 125 years. Yeah, sure, an oak tree fell on it....

Some of the wire I bought. Some I salvaged. The most durable wire fencing I found in a defunct mink operation.

To put together coops or cages, you need some special tools and fasteners. J clips tightly hold two wires together. You will want to remove clips once in a while.

There is the tool for that, two little sharp teeth on strong jaws. If you need a looser connection, pig rings work well with another special tool.

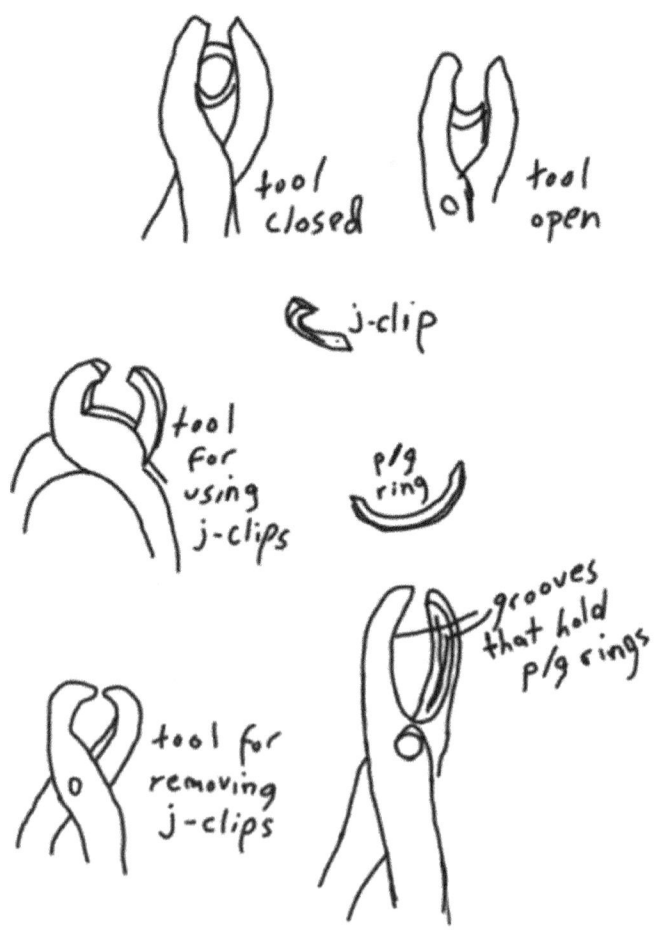

(There are a variety of rabbit coop or hutch designs. Most, in my opinion, are not long enough.)

Another consideration is that the housing be predator proof. When I had rabbits as a young girl, rats got into the cages and killed the three-week-old bunnies. If they didn't physically kill them, the stress apparently killed them. So - rat proof.

My daughter Sarah has horses and delivers them to various locations. She has brought back used rabbit hutches for me. The most recent was a well-built duplex into which I put two of my bucks. About a year and a half later, I found one of the bucks dead. He didn't have the usual mink attack markings. His mouth and nose were chewed away. So, suspecting mice, I cleaned up that side of the coop and buried the rabbit. The next morning the other buck was dead, same markings. I decided to take care of him after finishing chores.

As I finished, I saw a mink climb the coop and enter it - under the roof. The mink proceeded to try to haul the dead rabbit into the nest box. I called a friend who came over with his pellet gun. While he decided on his approach, the mink left the coop. We set a live trap, wedging the dead rabbit in as bait. Two hours later, the mink was in the trap. I had called my son-in-law and he took mink and trap up to a wildlife refuge thirty miles from here. A nicer end for that mink.

So, mink have long been a problem. Not a lot, but traumatic enough that I remember isolated incidents. Last year, around twilight, I checked the yard and noticed that I had left the gate open and five rabbits had been killed. Mink usually seem to hunt alone. Thinking that this one was still in the area, I set the live trap with the smallest victim, Maxine. A couple of hours later, the mink was in the trap along with Maxine. Not aware of any kind of alternatives, I filled a fifty-gallon barrel with water and dumped the trap with the contents into the barrel. There was one half inch of air above the water, and I decided to let the mink swim up for air until I had finished chores. He had drowned by the end of the half hour.

I wish I had known about the wildlife refuge at that time but I hadn't. He was only doing what mink do. They kill to eat but they also seemed to kill for fun.

(Before the execution water bath on 4/9/15, he was a beautiful animal but after he killed five of my fine rabbits, I couldn't let him go. Coat rich chocolate brown, jaw resting on Maxine, his prey, his mistake and his comfort. The water filled recycling barrel didn't go deep enough. But within a half hour he died after he had made trips to the top of the submerged cage.)

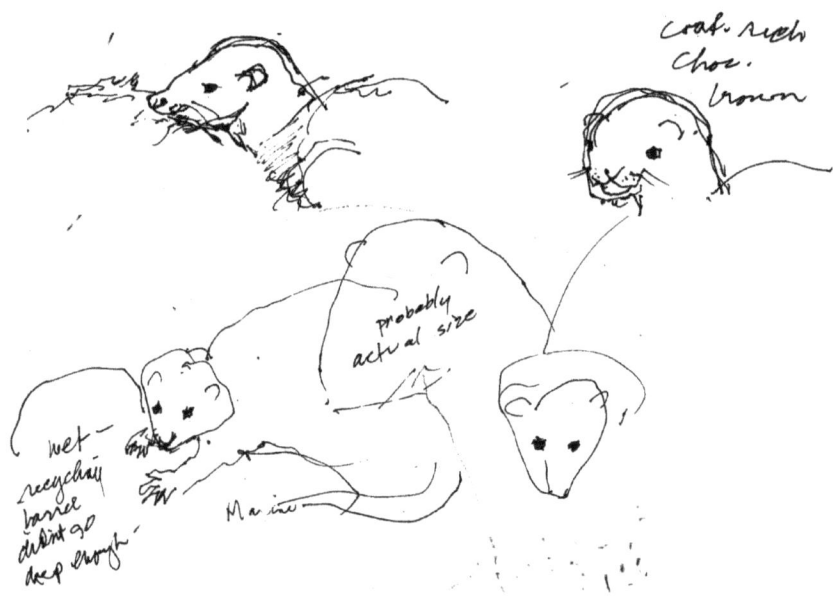

HEALTH AND WELLNESS

Getting to know your angora rabbit

In order to understand what is going on with your rabbits, you need to spend time not only working with them but just observing them at different times of the day. Adult rabbits seem to spend most of the day resting. Night and early morning are more active times. (Youngsters and juniors seem to be active all of the time.) If you check them only in the middle of the day, it is possible to misinterpret their body language.

Language

Each rabbit is an individual. Most will "follow the crowd" but not all. Some will urinate in the nest box, some will eat pellets and not oats (or vice versa), some are outgoing, some are reclusive; some will be a big pain to work on: chances are that one of those will have the most wool!

Picking up and carrying your Rabbit

Domestic rabbits retain their flight instincts. Any sudden or unexpected sounds, such as noisy children or a strange dog, could set the entire rabbitry into panic.

Approach your rabbit quietly. Removing a rabbit from a cage and carrying it are critical maneuvers. The rabbit's skin is very loose, so when you reach into the coop for him, grab a good fold of upper back skin just behind the neck with the other hand and arm. Immediately secure the animal's back legs, holding them closely against his body and yours.

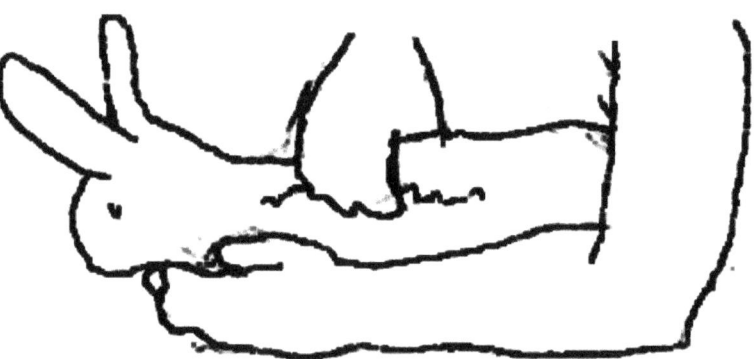

Sometimes when I am carrying a rabbit back to his coop, he will all of a sudden decide to launch off into space. Doing this, he can break his back and paralyze his legs. There is not much that you can do for this rabbit should it happen.

Wrapping a rabbit in a towel before carrying it may help the animal feel more secure and prevent you possibly from getting scratched - or you can put him in a five-gallon bucket with a lid at the ready.

Once in a long while a rabbit may break his own neck. A sudden, unexpected movement on the part of the rabbit himself can break the connections between the vertebrae. You'll know when this happens – your rabbit is now dead.

Some Numbers and Statistics

Temperature: 102°F to 103°F. Anything above may indicate a problem.

Normal pulse rate: 140 to 150

Respiration rate: 50 to 60

Longevity: An animal may reach ten or more years but more often around five or six.

Mortality: Worldwide mortality is around 20 to 25 percent annually and includes nest box deaths, kits born dead, adolescent deaths, and the loss of bucks and does.

Diet

When you purchase your angora rabbits, ask the seller for a few days' feed. Never change diet abruptly; any change in food must be done gradually. Mix the previous feed in larger to smaller proportions, over a week, when you will be feeding only your "new feed". Even different brands of pellets should not be introduced all at once. The first consideration in the diet is the pelleted feed. Corn should not be one of the major components in a feed for angoras. There are pellets without corn, but most feeds contain it.

Some rabbit breeders feed only pellets. I mix one-part whole oats with two or three parts pellets, and to this I add some black oil sunflower seed. You may find yourself adjusting this mix if you use it. If you have only one or two rabbits, you may want to use rolled oats instead of the whole oats. If wheat and/or barley is available, I like to add some of that to the mix.

Hay is desirable for the proper functioning of the angora rabbit gut. Timothy is the generally preferred grass hay, but other grass hays are good, too. Rabbits delight in getting alfalfa hay but limit the amount.

If you purchase your hay, make sure that it comes from a recent cutting, is not moldy, and does not contain woollypod milkweed or nightshade. It's probably best to avoid weedy hay.

Aside from woollypod milkweed and nightshade, I don't know what to list except for lily of the valley leaves, rhubarb leaves and tall yellow and white clovers. Rabbits are quite discriminating about their food;

they've probably inherited the ability to select what's good for them. Don't count on this, though!

Forages

Here in the Midwest, our wild rabbits adjust their diet with the seasons: they have to! Based on this, I very gradually increase the amount of fresh forage during the spring and summer.

By summer, I give a pretty good handful, but the rabbits should get only what they will readily eat. During the late fall and winter, fresh forages are no longer available, but I continue to give them a daily fresh treat. This might be apple or pear twigs, red and black raspberry cuttings and willow - alternated with pieces of carrot, apple, pineapple flesh and skin, mango, papaya, grapes, organic citrus peels. The following list of forages is based on what I find available in order, from the beginning of spring and on into summer:

Nettles

Dandelion

Violets

Strawberry leaves

Yellow dock

Garden thinnings

Plantain

Radish Leaves

Mustards

Arugula

Mulberry shoots & leaves

Red and black raspberry shoots and leaves

Comfrey (best dried)

Corn shucks and silk

Red and green sorrels

Hay type grasses

Broccoli

Only small amounts of the following:

Alfalfa

Red clover

Willow (contains salicylic acid, an aspirin compound)

Lettuces

Spinach

Cabbages

Lamb's quarters

You can most likely add to either list. Think about what rabbits eat in your garden! Give very small amounts of new forage.

Don't forget fresh water! In the winter snow may be a substitute, but offer fresh water. If the water freezes, replace the containers with the empty ones.

Supplements

Pelleted feeds supposedly contain all of the supplements necessary for good rabbit health. I rely upon that - to a degree – (but I add some oats - and wheat and/or barley if available - and sunflower seed for the oil). Earlier I provided salt spools; they were seldom used. The green forages that I feed when they are available are, I think, beneficial. They also reduce pellet and grain consumption.

Coprophagy

Part of the rabbit's diet for which you are not responsible is something the rabbit does daily for himself - he or she eats night feces. You might find these shiny little grape-like clusters (SAMPSON 1992, 112) on the floor of the coop or cage but most likely you will see the rabbit hunched over, eating these moist droppings directly from his or her anus. These are a source of B vitamins, some intestinal flora and a little protein. This daily eating of the night feces seems to be absolutely essential to the rabbit's digestive process. I have noticed that after a week or two without this self-feeding, the rabbit's health deteriorates; the first symptom is loss of weight.

I believe, though I haven't tried it, that feeding some night feces from a healthy rabbit to one "doing poorly" may help.

Thinking back to the few times when I had a rabbit who "just kept losing weight" perhaps not eating the night feces was at fault. With our recent emphasis on human gut health, our medical community has done similar procedures.

Reading the Evidence - Scatology

Probably the easiest way to determine an angora's state of wellness is by reading its droppings or scats. (SAMPSON 1992, 109)

Numbers one and two are most likely to be a mom with a litter of babies. Numbers nine and ten could be droppings from babies, but if they are from an adult, suspect wool block (or that they may not be getting enough water.)

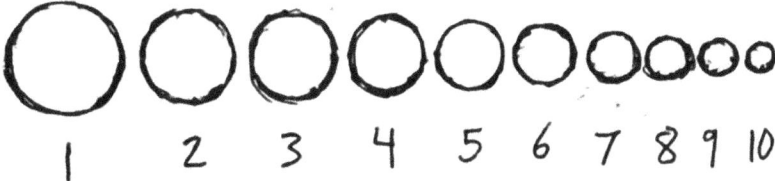

This appearance:

...can mean that the rabbit is getting rid of excess hair and that it is making its way through the digestive system. Check the rabbit's coat if the hair is loose - it needs to be plucked or clipped.

Wool Block

That gorgeous wool coat on the angora is the animal's greatest liability. When wool block develops, the animal may exhibit lack of interest or energy coupled with very small or non-existent scats; or hunched body posture and very small or no scats. Wool block can be a serious problem – see more information in the following section on enteric diseases.

There are a number of reasons for developing wool block:

1. Rabbits have no cough reflex. Both rabbits and cats groom themselves. Cats spit up hairballs. Rabbits cannot. This is why you need to be watchful.

2. An individual rabbit's digestive system may not be able to handle large amounts of ingested hair. This may be an inheritable trait.

3. Warm weather can result in earlier hair loosening.

4. Failure by the owner to groom regularly or to check the hair condition.

5. Grooming too often. The rabbit will always follow your grooming with its own.

6. Pseudo pregnancy which motivates the doe to pull out her hair for a nest.

7. Failure to remove all loose hair from the coat you have just plucked or clipped. Follow this hair removal with your comb and wire brush. Give six papaya tablets at this time; it will help that hair move through the digestive system.

Pasteurellosis – Associated Diseases

A number of different pathogens affect rabbits. The most prominent is the bacteria Pasteurella Multocida (TEMPLETON 1982, 166). It is found in most rabbitries. Vaccines for it have been developed and tried but to little effect. As its name implies, Pasteurella Multocida manifests itself in a number of ways. The most usual is respiratory. Sometimes other pathogens may also be present.

Pasteurellosis is the umbrella term for all of the various manifestations of Pasteurella Multocida.

Snuffles

Most common is snuffles. There is no such thing as a cold in rabbits. There may be sneezing which results from allergy to dust, mold or other nasal irritants, but if there is a whitish nasal discharge and wet front feet from wiping the nose, that is a sign of snuffles. This is highly contagious, but some animals seem not to be affected by this pathogen. Any affected animal should be isolated. You can treat it with an antibiotic but snuffles will usually return.

Pneumonia

Pneumonia is the successor to snuffles. If a rabbit is breathing with its mouth open and possibly its head back; the pink eye color in an albino rabbit is a bluish pink and the lips look bluish, you should suspect pneumonia. Pneumonia is a major cause of death in rabbits.

Abscesses

Abscesses occur whenever the rabbit's body mounts a defense against an infection by Pasteurella Multocida. The entrance is usually a cut or abrasion. You may first notice it as a hard lump, or not well-defined at this point. You may wish to inject some antibiotic under the skin (Sub-Q). Leave it for a couple of days. When you check it again, you may find that the hard lump has changed to a soft puss-filled lump. The abscess can now be lanced. To do this, clip the hair over and around the abscess, swab the area with alcohol, and lance the soft area. Have tissue or paper towels handy to collect the purulent material. Clean the emptied space with hydrogen peroxide, wipe it clean, and into that space squeeze some antibiotic. Check within a day or two to make sure that the lesion is healing from within.

Sore Hocks

Some of the most common abscesses are usually found on the back feet. Sparse hair growth on the pads of the feet may enable irritation and abrasion, creating what are called "sore hocks". If the rabbit doesn't move normally, suspect this problem. To treat, clean the area with hydrogen peroxide. Apply an antibiotic and wrap the foot with a gauze bandage. Older clean sheeting works, too. Provide clean bedding for the rabbit and change it and the foot wrapping every few days. Front feet may also be affected, but rarely.

Infections in a leg joint are the most difficult to clean out and help heal. A rabbit can live with an abscess for a long time and most likely will not pass the infection onto other rabbits.

Wry Neck

Another problem associated with Pasteurella Multocida is Torticollis or "wry neck". The rabbit holds its head to one side or the other; he may lose his balance. This is caused by an inflammation in the inner ear, probably following some respiratory problem. The rabbit may remain in this state for a long time, but it will get worse. There is not much that you can do to treat it. Culling is the most humane solution.

Metritis, Orchitis, Rabbit Syphilis

Diseases which affect reproduction are metritis, orchitis and rabbit syphilis. Metritis affects the doe. She does not conceive, and there may be a yellow-white discharge from her vagina. With orchitis, more rarely seen in the buck, testicles become infected and large and very warm. You may treat for these conditions with antibiotics, but never use a buck with orchitis for breeding.

Rabbit syphilis infects both does and bucks, and is caused by a different pathogen, treponema cuniculi, a spirochete.

This disease is characterized by blisters and red, raw sores on the genitals. In more serious cases, there are open sores and scabs around the eyes and nose. Dark field microscopy is the surest way to determine rabbit syphilis. Penicillin is usually the treatment.

Enteric Diseases

Enteric diseases are the other large group of rabbit diseases. At one time, it was thought that all diarrheal problems were the same disease, but now these problems are considered to be four separate diseases.

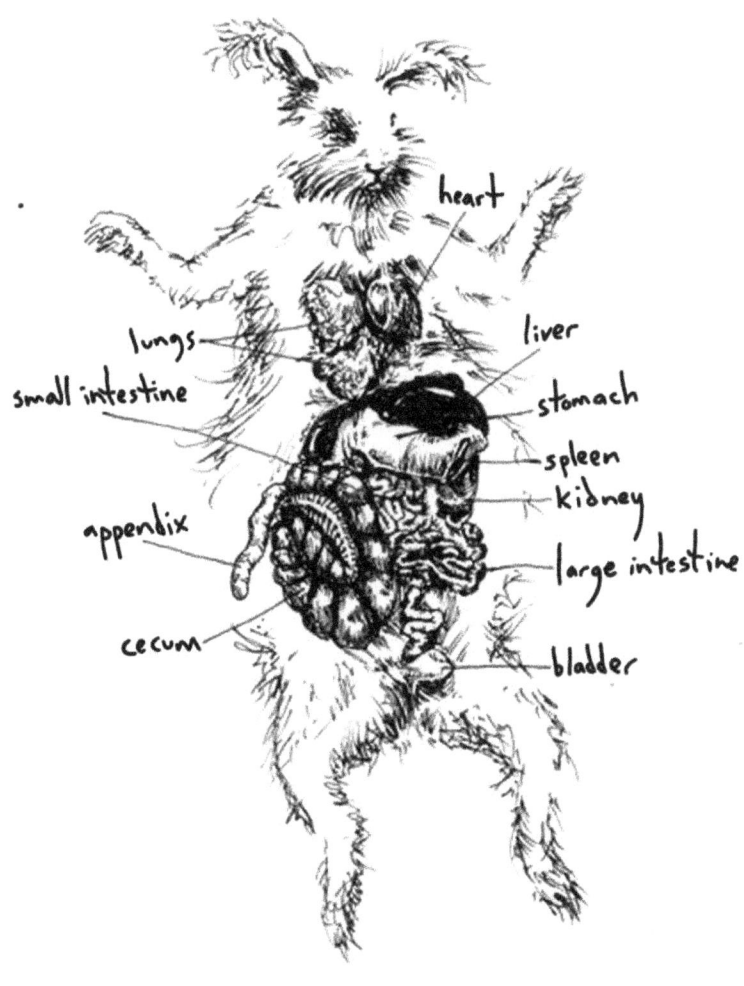

All can affect rabbits at different ages but one can think of them as mostly affecting rabbits between four and twelve weeks of age.

Mucoid Enteritis

A sometimes-overlooked problem associated with wool block is mucoid enteritis. All rabbits are vulnerable to wool block because no rabbit has that cough reflex; and because of the length of the hair, are more at risk.

Impaction is generally in the small intestine or at the entrance to the cecum; but I have, in a post-op investigation, found a stomach to be packed tightly with swallowed hair.

The rabbit sits in a pained hunched position, drinks large quantities of water, doesn't eat and has a watery diarrhea which may be almost black in color, has a nauseating smell and includes a yellow-brown mucus. The rabbit's belly will be swollen, gassy and hollow sounding when tapped. Pick the rabbit up and you will hear a sloshing sound. His ears will feel cool and he will often grind his teeth.

If you discover this early enough and start antibiotic injections (½ CC for each 9 pounds, later, less) you may be able to save him. Keep him warm - and good luck. I've never had any stay alive with this condition. Death is usually in three to five days.

If your rabbit is still eating and drinking, give him five or six papaya tablets. Original flavor is best. Also good are fresh or frozen pineapple skin and flesh. Fresh papaya is also good. Heat destroys these enzymes, so don't feed these things canned or cooked. These usually get the digestion moving, but an inch of cat hairball remedy administered orally should help. After an hour or two, give the rabbit another five or six papaya tablets.

If your rabbit is not eating or drinking, don't waste any time in treating him. Squeeze an inch or so of cat hairball remedy - even if salmon flavored is all you could find - into his mouth.

Wait an hour or two and offer any of the other treats mentioned above if the rabbit is not interested. Grind up papaya tablets to a powder. Mix with a couple of tablespoons of water and feed it to the rabbit with an eye dropper or a needleless syringe. Hopefully your rabbit still has a swallowing reflex.

This is a tricky operation. It's very easy to get the liquid into the lungs. Repeat this every two hours until you start seeing evidence of movement. Usually, the first scats are very small. Continue the treatment until the rabbit and its scats appear more normal.

I have read about surgical removal of hair blockage. This may be a remedy if the rabbit survives the anesthetic. I once lost a rabbit which had had the minimal dosage.

Enterotoxemia

Enterotoxemia was first described as a separate disease in 1978. Profuse diarrhea, dehydration and no interest in eating are all symptoms. These rabbits die within twelve to twenty-four hours. Post-op may reveal the presence of several bacteria, notably Clostridium Perfringens type E and Escherichia Coli. These produce toxins in the cecum, the large intestinal section between the small and large intestines.

Enterotoxemia is found more in rabbits which are fed low fiber diets. This seems to be a cyclic disease, most often affecting large herds. Overcrowding and lack of sanitation are also culprits. A broad-spectrum antibiotic such as Oxytetracycline added to the water may seem to "cure" the problem, but it usually returns when the antibiotic is discontinued.

Tyzzer's Disease

Tyzzer's disease is similar to Enterotoxemia with profuse diarrhea and rapid death. Microscopic investigation reveals salt-grain sized white spots in the liver, which are generally the bacterium Bacillus Pilliformis. No treatment has been found effective.

Coccidiosis - Intestinal

Coccidiosis is one of two types - intestinal and liver. Both are caused by a protozoan parasite which invades either the bile duct or the intestine. If one of the chimera protozoans infects the intestine, this is generally not a serious problem. To treat it, I have found the sulfa drug quinoxaline to be effective. It is a liquid. Add it to the rabbit's water, two tablespoons per gallon. Use this for two weeks. Some rabbitries periodically treat the entire herd.

Coccidiosis - Liver

Liver coccidiosis poses a different problem. This is Eimeria Stiedae, and shows up as white spots on the liver. Such a liver is not marketable or edible. If the infection is severe, it can kill the rabbit.

Diarrhea

Diarrhea is most often seen in growing rabbits. It may not always be a pathogen problem; it could be too much green forage, too sudden a change in diet, or there could be a problem with the pelleted feed. Make good grass hay available.

Viral Diseases

Myxomatosis

Myxomatosis is a viral disease in rabbits and may be transmitted to domestic rabbits by mosquitoes. There are two forms of the disease: the Fast-killing and the Chronic. All ages of rabbits are vulnerable.

With the rapid killing form, all you may notice are dead rabbits. With the chronic form, the face and head swell, the temperature may reach 105 to 106. Swollen genitalia verifies the infection. There is nothing effective against the virus. Years ago, myxomatosis was introduced into the Australian wild to kill off the local rabbits.

Tularemia

This is a disease which we heard about when I was a child. I remember that my mother was reluctant to cook wild rabbit "gifts" from local Nebraska hunters. Tularemia was first noted in Tulare County in California, carried by wild rabbits, squirrels and rats, and it is transmissible to humans. In the wild, mortality is almost 100 percent.

Rabbit hemorrhagic disease virus 2

First identified in France in 2010, cases have since been found in the US in Washington, Ohio and New York and the Southwestern States. It does not spread to other mammals and is not a threat to human health.

Internal Parasites– Tapeworm, Pinworm

When small rectangular white segments show up in a scat, you know your rabbit has a tapeworm. He may lose weight. Eventually you may see no more evidence. Dogs and cats are carriers for tape worms, so keep them out of the rabbitry.

Seeing 4 to 7 mm long slender worms in the scat are probably pinworms, not uncommon in rabbitries. Though they are not usually a problem, they can contribute to poor condition. They are found in the cecum and the large intestine, and sometimes around the anus. A pasty diarrhea indicates a heavy infestation.

The off-label Ivermectin is effective in ridding your rabbits of this parasite. (TEMPLETON 1982, 89) See dosage directions for hair mites. The most effective treatment is to use Ivermectin – 15 units on an insulin syringe for each 5 pounds of animal weight. (Half that amount has been shown to be enough.)

I have found cat flea powder to be effective for small patches. The vegetable fruit insecticide Sevin is also good.

Nosema or Encephalitozoonosis

Nosema or Encephalitozoonosis is caused by a protozoan parasite called Encephalitozoon cuniculi and is generally diagnosed only in postmortem exams. The parasite attacks the kidneys and sometimes the brain, causing neurological difficulties.

External Parasites

Wool Mites

If the rabbit skin feels greasy, and what looks like dandruff is present, your rabbit most likely has wool mites. The most common of the species is Cheyletiella parasitovorax parasite – or "walking dandruff". There is no dandruff in rabbits. What you see are about the size of a grain of sand and will try to avoid your inspection. An infestation of these beasties is called a mange and results in damaged hair follicles, greasy feeling wool and resultant matting. Mange is transferred from animal to animal via show tables, from tools used on other mite-infected rabbits, or transfer to other coops or cages. Mange is easily spread but there is no evidence that these Cheyletiellid Mites like human skin.

Ear Mites

You may not see them, but if your rabbit is shaking his head as if he's trying to get rid of something or if she is scratching her ear, suspect ear mites. Ear mites, or Psoroptic Mangemites are larger than wool mites, and they live and feed on the skin and blood serum around, and in, the ears of the rabbit.

To treat, drop drops of mineral or vegetable oil into the ear canal and gently squeeze the base of the ear. If there is a buildup of drowned mites etc., gently squeezing the base of the ear may present you with the evidence. Repeat this treatment as necessary. There are preparations with medication but I have not found these to be necessary. Ivermectin is the preferred treatment of the ear if heavily infested.

Fleas

The chances are that you will seldom encounter these, but if you do, use the mildest cat powder you can find. Sevin also works, but be sparing in your application of these powders - "What goes onto the rabbit goes into the rabbit" via self-grooming.

Warbles

This is something that I have not encountered, but if you find a lump it most likely is on the rabbit's neck or shoulders - around the chin or under the chin. Remove the hair from that area and take a good look at it. If you see a small hole at the top of the lump you are looking at the entrance of a bot fly, made for an egg, which turns into a larva - which develops into another botfly. Don't confuse this with an abscess; If you are patient, you will probably see some movement inside the lump. Enlarge the hole by massaging the lump until it expels the larva. Flush with hydrogen peroxide and apply an antiseptic.

Flaky Skin

There is no such thing as dandruff in rabbits. Poor diet, internal parasites, tapeworms, pinworms or most likely wool mites may be the problem. I discuss this in the external parasite section.

Fly Strike

Hopefully you will never encounter this, but if you hear flies buzzing and smell something really unpleasant, you need to check immediately. The flies that you hear are those that are used in forensic investigation and are called blue bottle or "bot" flies. These are attracted to necrotic flesh or something that may hint of it. This may be a wound that was not treated, or a diarrhea, or – rarely - a rabbit that has been sprayed upon by another rabbit. These flies gather en-masse and start doing their best to get rid of the affected rabbit. (or just incubating more flies?!) They lay their two to three mm long eggs singly or in clusters.

In a short time, these eggs will become wriggling maggots which will start to feed on the rabbit's flesh. In three or four days, the rabbit may die from the poison that accompanies this fly assault, but you can treat it if you get at it right away.

To treat it, you:

1. Clip all of the hair (wool) that contains the eggs and larva. Clip all of the wool down to the skin. If you see movement, hatched maggots are trying to escape your scissors.

2. When you think you have removed all of the hair infested, wait a bit and check again.

3. Cleanse the area with hydrogen peroxide and spray the rabbit with a fly spray. I have used something called Catron which kills eggs, larva and flies; but it is very toxic.

4. Check the rabbit carefully; maggots will use whatever entrance into the body that is moist – usually, the anal/genital recesses. You may find maggots there hiding from your investigations.

5. Keep this animal nearby so that you can check it often. You may have missed a few eggs or larva.

6. An injection of antibiotic may be useful to treat any underlying cause and to promote healing.

Fly strike that has not been taken care of for a day or two will probably be the yuckiest situation you may ever encounter. Cleaning this up may result in saving your rabbit but it may take a month to recover. Years ago, I discovered a fly trap unit that consisted of a special quart jar lid and a small bottle of yellow liquid.

The special lid allowed flies entrance but denied them exit. The yellow liquid turned out to be unnecessary. (I found this out after having used it - one tsp for each half quart of water.) Most important was the addition of about two oz of fresh (or frozen fresh) meat. This rots and attracts just the bot flies. I put this trap out whenever the weather turns warm. When the jar gets full of trapped flies, dig a hole. Dump in half of the jar's contents and cover it well. Add replacement water to your jar trap. This is an unpleasant job, but it's some insurance against fly strike.

Ringworm (Favus)

Ringworm is a fungal disease. It is called ringworm because the hair is often lost in a circular pattern over crusty shallow sores that show up typically on rabbits faces or feet. There are several species of fungi that can affect rabbits. Some may be transmissible to other rabbits and/or humans. This disease is most commonly found in the nursing young but can affect adult rabbits as well. When handling these animals, wear disposable gloves and after handling them, wash and sanitize everything that has been in touch with them. The least expensive topical treatment is ordinary iodine. Check with your vet for further information.

Other Maladies and Fixes

Ventilation, sanitation and observation are three of the most important factors involved in disease control.

Sometimes the urine is quite red - no worry, it may have to do with the feed, or it may be an individual thing. Rabbits absorb calcium efficiently and excrete the excess, which is calcium carbonate; this may form deposits on the floor or sides of the cage.

Cold weather is generally not a problem but one needs to make sure that the wool is long enough for the rabbit to keep warm. Pluck only what is the loose outer coat. I once plucked too much off of a favorite bunny and dressed him in a sweatshirt. He chewed it off and succumbed to the cold. I should have taken him and kept him indoors.

Ears have frozen in very cold weather. They will turn red, swell, and feel very warm. Eventually the swelling will go down, and the frozen parts will dry up and fall off. I don't know of any treatment.

Warm and humid weather is harder for angoras than cold weather, although I'm always amazed at how well they manage the heat. When it is very warm, jugs of cold water in their coops gives them some relief. When I do shows, and it's hot, I have a towel-wrapped cold pack on my lap between the rabbit and me.

Urine Burn or Hutch Burn

This is generally not a serious matter but if your rabbit is uncomfortable and this gets worse, clip away the soiled wool, gently wash the skin and clean it with hydrogen peroxide. Rub on some antibiotic. If this continues and larger areas get wet, there may be a urinary problem for which your vet may have a remedy. Make sure that the cage floor and any bedding are kept clean. Urine burn may attract botflies (see fly strike).

Weeping eyes

In English and German angoras, long hair may simply be the problem - irritating the eyes. Clip it. If you see some cream-colored exudate from the eye(s) there is an infection. Your veterinarian will have an ophthalmic ointment available which I have used, and which needs to be applied three times a day.

Buck Teeth – Malocclusion

If you notice a rabbit which is trying to eat but doesn't seem to be able to pick up his food, check his teeth. Rabbits have most of their teeth toward the back of the jaw. There are two pairs of premolars and three pairs of molars in the bottom jaw. (SAMPSON 1992, 85)

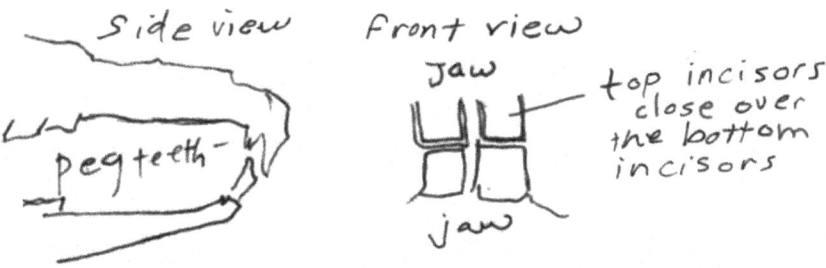

There are three pairs of premolars and three pairs of molars in the top jaw. The top and bottom jaw each have one pair of incisor teeth.

The top jaw has an extra pair of tiny peg teeth - right behind the incisors. These little teeth serve a unique purpose; to keep the bottom teeth filed down. Rabbits' bottom teeth keep growing, just as our fingernails do, and these little teeth provide a block to the bottom incisors. If these peg teeth are missing, the bottom incisors will keep growing and will need trimming. Use a wire cutter or pliers and clip them to normal length.

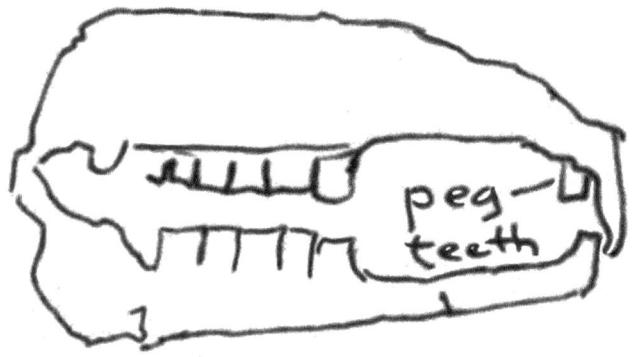

Another cause of buck teeth is the length of the bottom jaw. If it is longer than the upper jaw and the bottom incisors meet or cover the incisors in the upper jaw, these bottom teeth will continue to grow because there is nothing which limits their growth.

There again, they need to be clipped. Malocclusion is most likely genetically inherited. Do not use these animals for breeding.

Fur Chewing – Hair Pulling

Fur chewing and hair pulling are two different things. Fur chewing happens most often with juvenile rabbits grouped together in a cage. It could indicate a nutritional need, but more often I think it is a matter of boredom. Putting something like a tin can in the coop may help. If you notice patches of missing hair or wool on some in the group, the perpetrator will have his or her full coat. Isolate him for a while.

It is not always the case, but I associate hair pulling with the adult doe, who may or may not have a companion. She is going through a false, or pseudo pregnancy, and is intent upon building a nest. If she has a companion, she may pull some of her hair too. If you get to it early enough and the pulled hair does not contain a lot of hay or other bedding, you may salvage it and use it for yarn or felt.

Woollypod Milkweed Poisoning

Years ago, I had read about this in Cheek, Patton and Templeton's <u>Rabbit Production,</u> so from reading that, I was always very watchful when feeding hay or forage. Dried woollypod is a unique yellow-green color, easily distinguishable. https://www.minnesotawildflowers.info/flower/woolly-milkweed

Woollypod Milkweed - John Rusk May 2017 Licensed under
the Creative Commons Attribution 2.0 Generic License

With a recent hay cutting, not thinking at all about woollypod poisoning, one morning I found one of my rabbits with his legs splayed out and his head down on the floor of the cage.

I checked with Rabbit Production, and there it was, with illustrations. Woollypod milkweed contains a neurotoxin which had affected this rabbit. Monarch butterflies lay their eggs on this plant, and the hatched caterpillars are immune to the poison. Birds learn this.

To treat this, I used shallow feed and water dishes, supporting the head if it was necessary. I knew that I hadn't fed it any milkweed, but it must have been discolored and in old hay. After a couple of weeks, the rabbit had thrown off the poison.

Ketosis

Years ago, I found my beautiful black chinchilla angora dead in her coop. I hadn't noticed anything amiss, so I decided to do a post-op. I could hardly believe how much yellow fat there was packed around her internal organs. She had died from ketosis, a condition in which fat developing in the liver interferes with the normal metabolic processes and with the breakdown of fat into metabolizable energy. This causes ketone bodies to be produced.

In warm weather, ketosis is most commonly seen in does which are pregnant with a large litter. She may have difficulty delivering her young. If you suspect a large litter, start giving her calcium and glucose supplements. A daily handful of broccoli a week before a kindling would supply the calcium. One cc of glucose syrup or molasses given orally should supply the glucose. You may wish to consult your vet for this.

Mastitis

If a doe has a new litter and doesn't seem to feel like eating, check her teats (mammary glands). If they feel warm and red and, possibly hard, she has mastitis. Her temperature will be elevated.

This is time to intervene. I usually give a combiotic under the skin (SubQ) but injecting it into a muscle will get the medication more quickly to the site where it is needed. Three days of antibiotics should suffice.

If the doe lets her kids nurse while you are treating her, they are doing what they need to do. Don't foster these babies to another doe. The young will transfer the bacteria to her. If you need to feed them, use goats' milk as a substitute. Use an eye dropper or a doll bottle and nipple.

How do the teats become infected?

The nest box itself may be to blame. Before the doe kindles, make sure that the nest box has good drainage and/or plenty of absorbent material. Straw or grass hay are good. Don't use wood chips. They attach to mom's wool and she ingests too much hair removing them.

The nest should stay clean and dry for the first few days after the babies are born. Mom licks them clean, and her licking encourages urination as they nurse. This lasts for only five to ten minutes! After a week, change the bedding 'if necessary'. Don't add the soiled wool back to the nest: hopefully, you have stored and labeled some of her wool for this purpose, and there should be some wool still clean from that first nest.

Cancer, Uterine

There are several different forms of cancer in rabbits. It's not widely considered to be important because most rabbits are not kept long enough for cancer to show up. With rabbitries, as with most livestock operations for which production is the chief goal, this means that the majority of the breeding animals are female. We as angora breeders keep the does for several years and see uterine cancer progress in some of our animals from the age of two. By the time a doe is five or six years old, there is about an 80 percent chance that she will have cancer. She may do quite well, but if the cancer metastasizes and spreads to other organs, she will lose weight and die. Whether or not she has had young does not affect these statistics. Genetics may influence them.

Young Doe syndrome

A doe has just had a fine litter of babies and everything seems to go well - but between six and ten days you might find her dead in the coop. There are a couple of things that can cause this - bacterial infection in the mammary glands may spread throughout her blood system and kill her - or it may be Enterotoxemia.

To avoid this second problem, start restricting feed during the gestation and after kindling. As the babies start to grow and she needs to produce more milk, cautiously add more feed, perhaps an ounce more each day. Make sure that she has water and grass hay.

If she is a doe who has left orphans, don't foster them to another doe. Bottle-feed them for a week or two with goat milk or perhaps a kitten formula. Use a doll bottle or a needleless syringe. After a week, add some baby oatmeal and a bit of molasses to the goat or cat milk.

THE ENTERPRISE

Harvesting the Wool

The French angora rabbit has a wool pattern that grows year-round, but every two or three months the outer coat gets loose and should be removed. The rabbit himself/herself will do much of that.

Rabbits are like cats in that if they are healthy, they groom themselves. (During a night storm, two of my young bucks got out. By morning, they were a mess, having fought and got muddy. I put each back in his own coop; by evening, both were clean again.)

However - unlike cats, rabbits do not have a cough reflex, and that swallowed hair can create "wool block". There are ways of treating it (See the Health and Wellness chapter) but it's best not to have to.

When the rabbit stops eating, or when the droppings are either very small or non-existent, hair may be collecting in the digestive system; so that hair must come off. I prefer to pluck - and that goes easily after some practice. Plucked fiber produces a yarn that doesn't shed, so it's only plucked fiber that I use for my yarns.

When harvesting, be very particular about keeping the fiber clean. Use a wire brush first, then a metal comb. Any hay or dirt or other foreign matter will show up later in your product.

Check to see if you can easily pull a few hairs.

With a bit of practice, you can pull more hairs at once.

Fiber that is clipped (I use an embroidery scissors) will most likely contain a good number of short hairs from the next coat growing in, and these will shed out in your yarn.

When I harvest, I create six piles of fiber, each intended for different use:

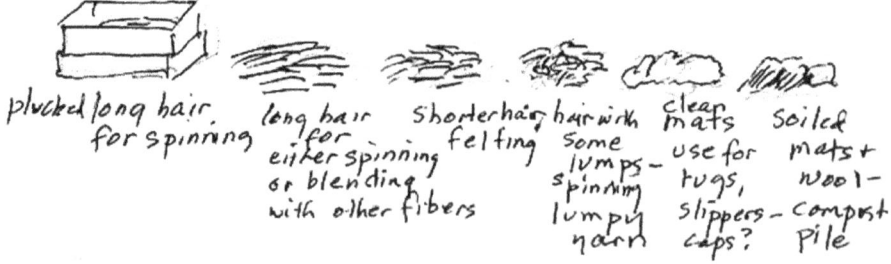

plucked long hair. for spinning

long hair for either spinning or blending with other fibers

Shorter hair felting

hair with some lumps - spinning lumpy yarn

clean mats use for rugs, slippers - caps?

soiled mats + wool - compost pile

Long, even fibers will be best for spinning into yarn. I keep this fiber in a shoebox. Keep colors separate.

When plucking fiber for spinning, I place it in shoeboxes with the root ends all in one direction. The ends of the fibers contain a very small amount of oil, and this seems to facilitate a smooth transition from lock to lock. Other grades of hair should be packaged and labeled clearly as to intended use.

- Short fibers will usually be carded and used for spinning or for felting.
- The small mats might be used for novelty yarns, and also for some felts, cat toys etc.
- The large mats will be useful for rugs and possibly slippers.
- If the hair is dirty or stained, or otherwise unusable, it will be used as compost.

So - I do use it all. Kept dry and clean - and free of fiber moths - angora doesn't seem to age. But, put it in a compost pile and it quickly disintegrates.

A note: When clipping, particularly where there are dense mats, make sure that the old mats close to the skin are removed. This is tricky, but a metal brush and comb help. Waiting two or three weeks for the new hair to grow in will make getting rid of this old hair easier! If you don't get rid of the old hair, you will find mats in the same places next time you harvest.

Removing Mats

Brush and comb the coat. When you locate a mat:

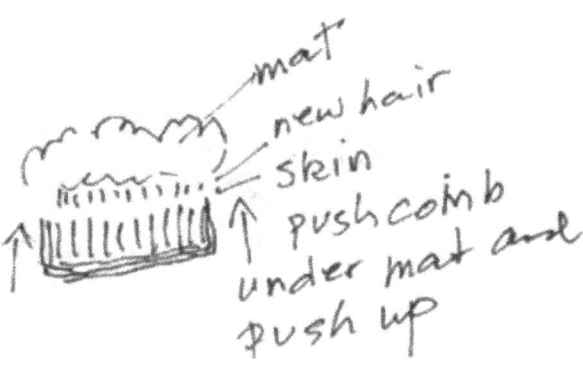

With a small sharp scissors, make short, cautious cuts. You don't want to clip the rabbit's skin.

Spinning

My First attempts at Spinning

A tip learned from experience: If you want a motorized spinning wheel, you will probably want one with variable speed.

Single ply angora yarn, I learned, falls apart. Two-ply seems best. Mittens knitted from this 100 percent angora shrank rather much, so reluctantly I heeded the advice I had received years before...it was from a Swiss angora yarn business owner: "100 percent angora doesn't work for yarns!" I ordered nylon to blend with the angora. So, I came up with a yarn that is 90 percent angora and 10 percent nylon. I like to spin "from the lock" - and this results in more "halo"- so one ply is 100 percent angora and the second is 80 percent angora - but carded with 20 percent nylon. This yarn is still the majority of my production and varies a bit in weight depending upon intended use.

My Spinning Technique

Two-Ply Yarn

To make usable yarn, you will need to twist together two "plies" that have been separately spun. By "ply" I mean a length of twisted fiber. The first ply will be 100 percent angora and the second will be 80 percent angora with 20 percent nylon.

Spinning the first Ply

If you are using a pedal–powered wheel as I use, first make sure that the wheel is "strung" - string the thin loop of cord around both wheel and bobbin.

"Prime" the bobbin by wrapping a few turns of a bit of string or starter yarn. Pull out a bit of that starter yarn and start pedaling a little bit to start twisting the yarn that is in your hand. Pick up a slim cluster of loose fiber in your hand and lay it alongside the yarn that is twisting so that the fiber starts twisting with the yarn that is already on the bobbin. Keep on pedaling as the yarn goes in, and keep on pulling from the little wad that you have in your hand.

The 100 percent angora first ply will be spun "from the lock" either directly from the rabbit or from a loose pile of locks previously harvested. The resulting ply will end up on a bobbin.

'Lock' in the spinning world means a loose tuft of fiber as it has been pulled from the rabbit - relatively loose, clean, not tangled, and ready to feed onto the spun fiber already on the bobbin.

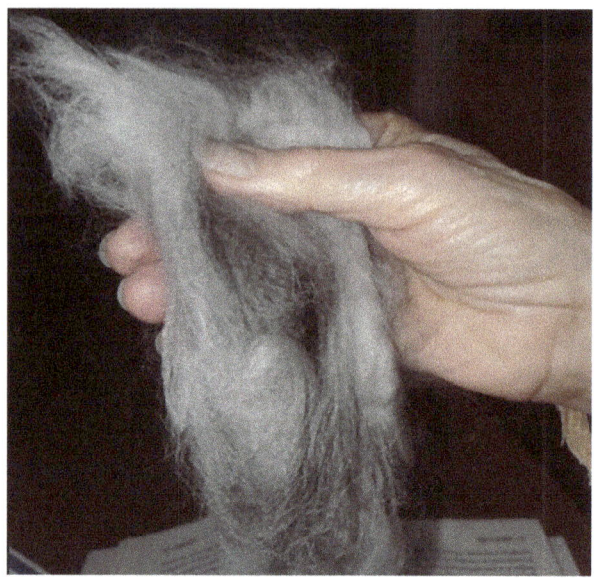

Try to keep it as uniform as possible. When you just about come to the end of the first clump, put in the next handful, and repeat. That's about all there is to it. Try to keep the same amount of fiber going through the bobbin so that your yarn is even, but it will take a bit of practice to do that. And if it's not too even, don't be too concerned about it because you will always double twist your strand later on.

You can control the amount of twist you apply. It is very easy to overtwist, because the yarn twists more easily than it draws itself in. Some practice is needed. To check the amount of twist, withdraw what you have spun, let it hang in the air, and whether it's a single ply or a double ply the yarn will double back on itself if overtwisted.

Note the direction your wheel is spinning! You will spin both plies with the wheel spinning in the same direction.

Spinning the second Ply

For the second ply, on a second bobbin, use carded angora, 80 percent angora and 20 percent nylon, and spin "from the strip". Prime the bobbin and start spinning as with the first ply, feeding carded angora/nylon strip onto that second bobbin.

Spin with the wheel in the same direction as you spun the first ply.

Twisting the Plies together

To twist the plies together, place onto a rack, conveniently at your feet, both bobbins, one filled with your 100 percent angora ply and the second filled with your 80 percent angora / 20 percent nylon ply.

Prime the bobbin with some starter yarn as when creating plies, and draw as before, the starter yarn out through the bobbin center hole. Lay the two-ply strands onto the three to four inches of the loose end of the starter yarn and pedal slowly at least two or three rotations as you have done before with single plies.

Once the two plies are firmly spun onto the starter yarn, reverse your wheel direction and spin in the direction opposite that used to make the plies. This will set the twist. As you spin, the fiber will be drawn into the bobbin hole, twisting as it is drawn in.

Angora blends well with other fine fibers such as alpaca, merino and some other lamb's wools, silk, kid mohair and tencel. For garments such as vests, sweaters and so on, the addition of other fibers can add interest and keep the garment from being too warm for indoor wear.

In sizing mittens, I need to allow for some shrinkage. Part of that shrinkage, I think, is from the way the smooth angora fibers work out of the yarn, creating that "halo" effect. Mittens, toe warmers and tams are my most popular knitted items. I rely on a couple of friends for most of that knitting; they don't make even minimum wage but seem to enjoy knitting with my yarns.

Using the shorter Fiber - Felting

I digress here for a moment to describe the method I have developed and found useful for the process of felting French angora.

I have long admired articles of clothing such as hats, vests and jackets made of felt. Many of these were first hand-knitted and then felted, but some were made directly from felted fabric. I'd never seen anything made from felted angora but I figured it was worth a try.

So, felting seemed a promising, logical solution to using the shorter fiber. But how? The hair is slippery, it doesn't have those barbs that enable wool to felt easily... Oh, I did find some instructions for making small sheets of angora felt. The layering was pretty much the same, but it was worked with the hands on a waist - high surface.

This process for felting angora didn't work for me, so I tried the method used for lambswool.

Since my objective was larger sheets of felt, I used my drum carder, which carded strips 7" by 22" in size.

Each layer would be roughly square and would require three of those strips.

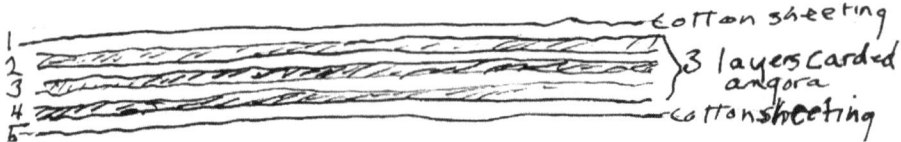

Layering the sheeting and the carded bats as I've illustrated, I was then instructed to pin or stitch the five layers in place. For flat, smooth felt - which was my objective - all directions called for two pieces of cotton or cottonblend sheeting plus three layers of carded wool. The middle-carded layer was to be cross-wise to the top and bottom up-and-down oriented layers.

I prepared each separate stack of material to be felted by first putting one piece of cotton sheeting down on a flat work surface (I used a ping-pong table) and then laid onto that the first layer of carded wool strips oriented up and down.

So... I used three strips, making sure there was no break between the strips. I laid on top of that the second layer oriented crosswise, and then the third layer up and down.

Subsequently, I placed the last piece of cotton sheet on top of the third layer of wool.

Thus assembled, I needed to secure the resulting five layers together by sewing long-lasting stitches or by pinning.

The next step was to sprinkle or soak the assembly with water and soap (or detergent) and then process it to accomplish the felting portion of the process - that is, entangling the individual fibers on a mass scale.

How would I felt this? I first tried to felt it by laying the assembly on the basement floor and spent some time pressing on it with my feet by running in place. This rearranged the fibers, but did not felt them.

So - I tried a couple of other approaches and prepared additional five-layer pieces, one with stitching and another with pinning. I then rolled each up like a jelly roll and tied it in several places to keep it together. I then put each roll in hot water in my washer, weighed it down with bath towels and let it soak overnight. In the morning, I was to start the washing machine on gentle and repeat this wash part of the cycle until I could feel the felting... At this point, I was to finish the cycle with rinsing and spinning.

The result was felt but not smooth - the pins and stitches held the wool in place but rolling produced ridges.

It finally occurred to me that, because angora is slippery, I needed to let it slide forward. Preventing this sliding during the rolling process would result in ridges (D'oh!) in the manner of corduroy writ large. I needed to let it slide forward.

No pinning, no stitching, just tightly rolling the assembly from near me to the far end, then pulling the roll into a pantyhose leg at one end. Turn the roll around and pull a second leg onto the roll. Secure it with ties, and soak and agitate the roll as before. That worked!

The felt on the far end turned out thinner but usable. Eventually I figured out that tucking under the ends of the crosswise layer made the edges more even with the body of the felt piece and kept stray hairs from pulling the entire piece out of shape.

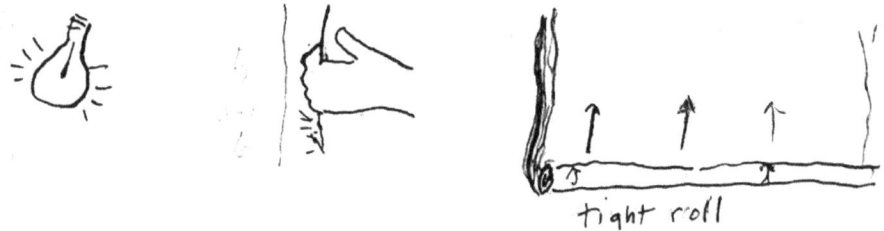

tight roll

Refining the Felting Process

I was, years later, still trying to figure out how to eliminate the occasional ridges and lumps. I thought I didn't have enough angora wool for the two sheets I was planning to make. I then considered using some alpaca - which is also a hollow, lightweight fiber - and the 15 percent to 25 percent addition of alpaca seemed to tame the angora. This made more of the entire sheet usable for insoles.

If alpaca is not available, the addition of some merino wool or nylon will also help to tame the angora. However, the addition of these fibers does not add to the warmth of the final product in the same way that the alpaca does. Nylon is less warm than the natural wools, among them, first and foremost angora with its superior hollow core.

What follows is the method I now use for making flat felt sheets of angora – alpaca mix.

Preparing the angora with alpaca for felting

1. You will need about 4 half-ounces of angora for each felted sheet, two cotton or cotton polyester sheets, dimensions of about 28" by 36", about one ounce of alpaca, three pantyhose legs or long stockings of different sizes, and a few nylon ties.

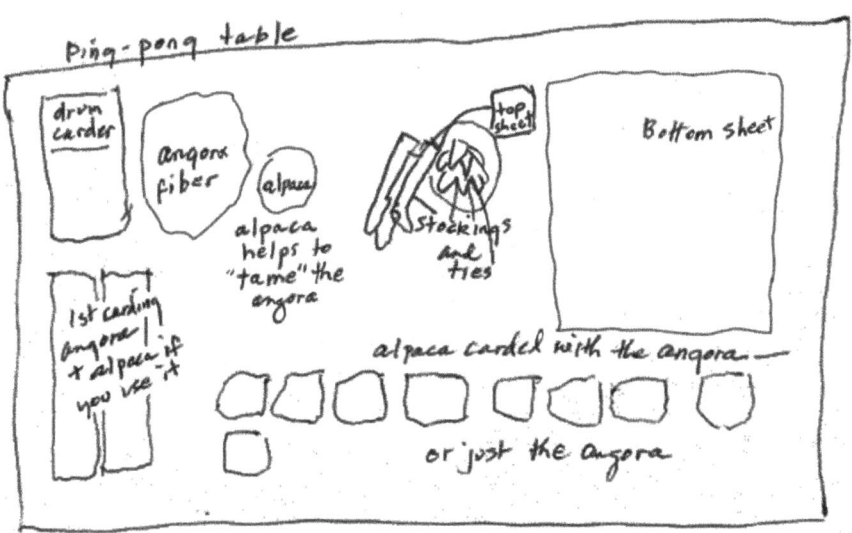

2. Card all of the angora - make sure that there is no debris in the wool - and make 9 half-ounce piles of carded angora. Card the alpaca, too, and divide it into nine little piles to use with the angora.

3. Card a second time as follows:

Lay down the first cotton sheet - allow for about 8" near you. Card the first of three angora piles; add the alpaca as you card if you are using it. Place the 1st carded strip vertically, about 3" from the left edge of the sheeting, and about 8" from the bottom of the sheet. Card piles number two and three and add them to that first layer, overlapping each strip so that there are no gaps.

4. Card, in turn, piles four, five and six with the addition of the alpaca. Lay each layer cross-wise over the first (vertical) layer, again overlapping the strips.

5. Finish the batt preparation by carding piles seven, eight and nine, as you did the previous two layers, and lay them vertically on the 2nd horizontal layer. Again, overlap the strips by just a little bit.

6. Tuck in any stray hairs in the margins.

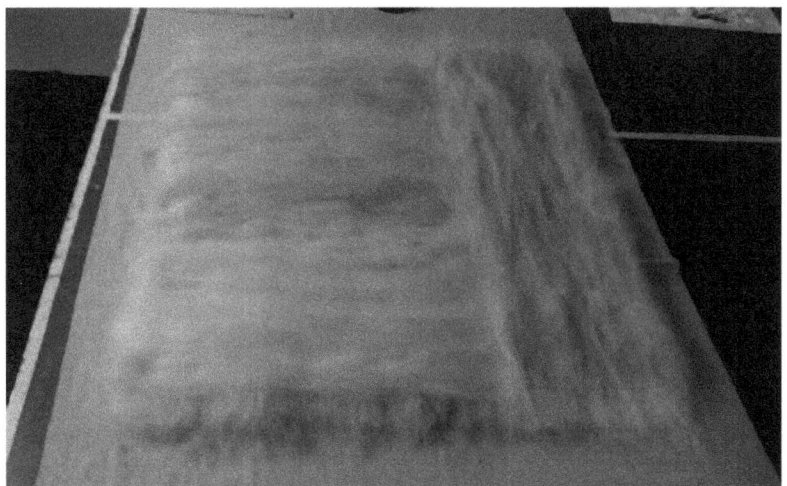

7. Fold up the cotton sheeting close to you, forming a tight roll around which you will roll the entire assembly. You may want to enlist some help for this.

Roll the piece as tightly as you can. Pull the assembly toward yourself as you work.

8. When you have finished the rolling, have available the three pantyhose legs (or long stockings).

9. Using the stocking with the largest opening - it should be about the same width as the end of the roll, pull the stocking down the length of the angora roll. Turn the roll around.

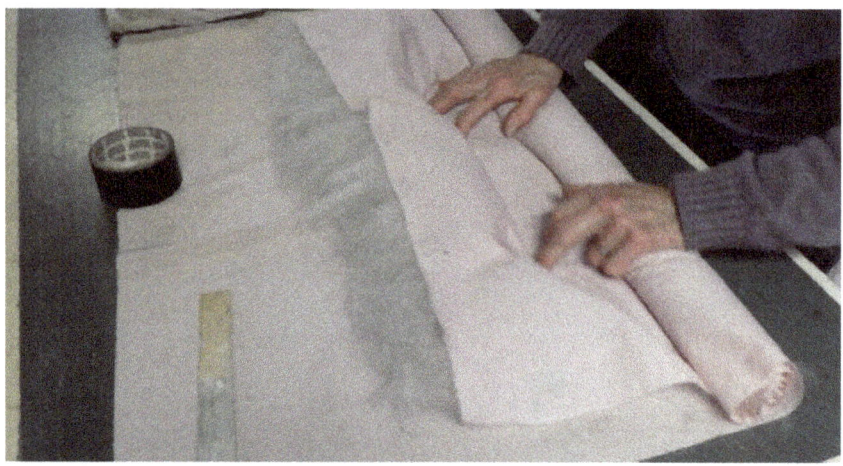

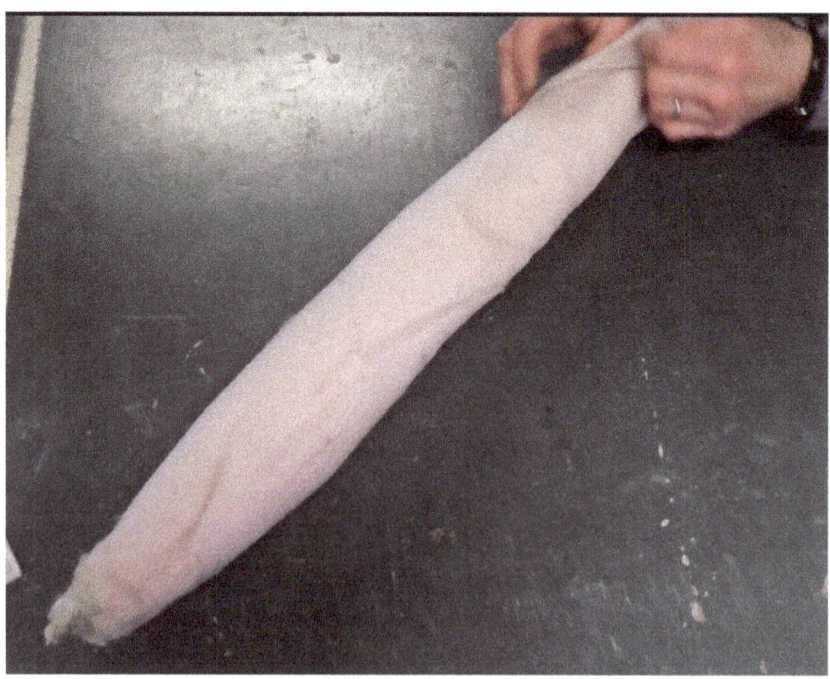

10. Use the middle-sized stocking for the second cover. It will be a little bit tighter. Again, pull it down and turn the roll around.

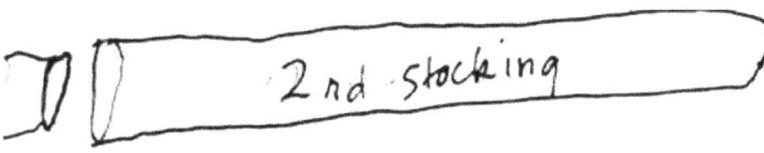

11. Use the smaller stocking for the outer cover.

You may need to squeeze the roll to accomplish this - the roll needs to feel firm. You don't want the assembly to have room to move around.

12. Done - tie with nylon ties in three or four places.

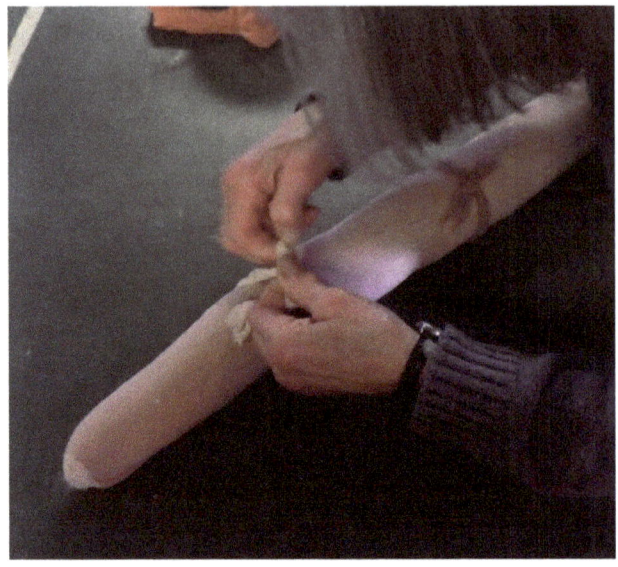

Now to felt your piece: you can felt one or more pieces at the same time. I usually felt two rolls at once.

1. Make sure your washer is on gentle cycle, and fill to the small load level with hot water. Place the prepared rolls in your washing machine. Add detergent or soap and enough hot water to cover the rolls and a couple of bath towels (which should hold the rolls under the water). Leave to soak overnight.

2. After the soaking, remove the towels. Repeat the gentle wash cycle until you can feel the roll harden. If you can, check one end to see if it has visibly felted. It can take from fifteen minutes to an hour. That depends upon the wool itself.

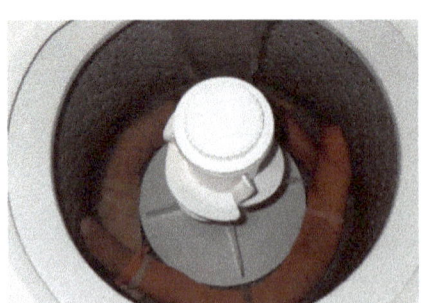
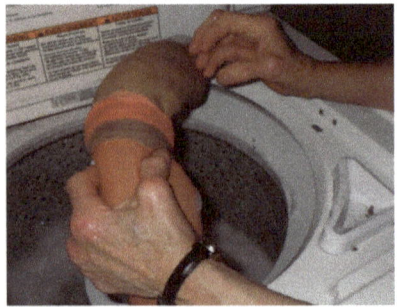

3. Finish the "gentle" cycle. I add an extra rinse.

4. Remove the rolls, one at a time, and stretch them over the top of the washer. Stretch (tenter) it from opposite corners and from side to side.

Finished felt, unrolled, to be tentered

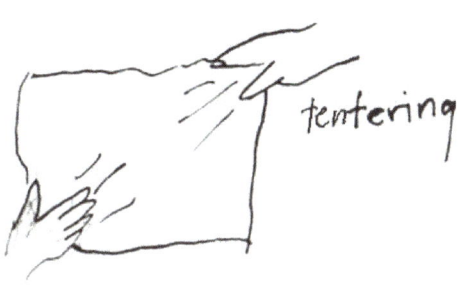

tentering

Remove loose fiber (a brush works) and hang your washed and rinsed piece(s) where there is good air circulation. If there is a breeze outside, it will dry quickly. Don't put it "wet" into the clothes dryer: it may continue to felt.

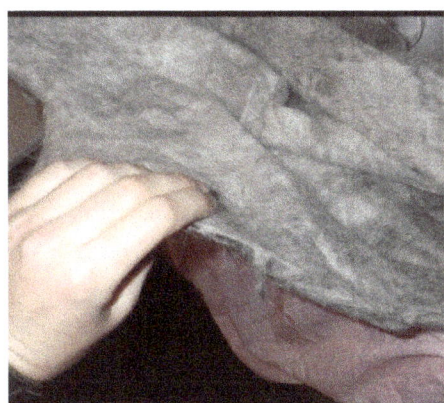

Thoroughly rinse the outer cloths and the towels, and hang them up to dry.

If you do not have a top loading washer or access to one, I don't know what to advise. Possibly soaking the prepared roll in a bucket of hot water with detergent, and then agitating it. Use your hands, potato masher, or one of those hand laundry aides - like a plunger with holes in it. When the rolls are firm, rinse thoroughly, stretch and dry the pieces.

If you do not have a drum carder, I think you can still make sheets of felt. Spread the fiber evenly and thinly onto cotton sheeting. If you have some webbed fiber, mix that in - it will help to speed the felting process. You will probably need to experiment as to the depth of the fiber you are laying on the sheeting. Cover with the 2nd piece of sheeting and roll, soak, agitate, and rinse it as I have previously mentioned.

You can try hand cards if you have them. I don't find them to be of much use for 100 percent angora.

Felt Projects

My first projects were angora yarn knitted into mittens. When someone suggested to me that I make insoles making felt from the shorter fiber, it seemed to be a reasonable idea.

100 percent angora does not felt easily, so it was a lot of trial-and-error before I managed to produce flat and even sheets of felt. Insoles are now my most popular item. Now I had found ways to use the long and the short and clipped wool.

What was I to do with the lumpy stuff? Cat Toys, clothes, drier balls, ornaments…

As for the large soft mats, they make wonderfully warm and soft rugs. Dirty mats and fiber make good compost. So, one can use all of the angora fiber.

Felt Insoles

The felting method that I described in detail is what I use for insoles.

To make thicker insoles, I've tried using five carded layers, but it's better to instead add a bit more fiber to each of the three layers.

Using this method, I've felted a number of different fiber blends - a 50/50 wool/angora blend is good for slippers - I've made those with angora lining, using the angora felt that's lightweight. Angora/merino is a lovely blend - suitable for hats, vest, jackets.

Angora/merino, angora/kid mohair and angora/alpaca are all good blends. One can blend angora with coarser fibers, but it's a little less desirable: The coarse fiber will be dominant.

One might think the baby hair, clipped at about ten weeks, would not be suitable for felt. It is difficult to work with, but it makes a 100 percent felt that is perfect for jackets and trousers for gnomes or dolls.

What can one make from felt scraps?

Consider - it's light-weight, it's warm, some scraps are fairly large, it takes dye well. Little things, like hearts, are very versatile - dyed red, they can be used as jewelry (stuffed or not), on greeting cards, as Christmas tree ornaments, with gold thread for hanging. Larger, heavier pieces can be used for baby mukluks (directions and patterns in the appendix). One can also piece scraps together for larger items. The felt rabbit is courtesy of Mary Walchuk.

In this age of 'synthetic everything', we don't see or even think about clothes moths. But they are still around, and they like natural fibers. So, if you stuff toys, or pillows or such with scraps, be aware that moths may find them. Remember cedar chests? They were used partly as protection against moth damage.

Another felted Project - Cat Toys

Cat toys are another example of 'making lemonade when life gives you lemons'.

I'd had an angora sweater knitted for a friend of a daughter-in-law. After she received it, she didn't want it. She thought it was too expensive to wear, so my daughter-in-law put it on the top shelf in her closet. Her cat climbed to that top shelf and chewed a one-inch hole in a sleeve. I had an AHA moment: Cat Toys from angora!

Felting little balls of lumpy fiber, then cutting them open and filling them with catnip was the answer.

There are always scraps left from cutting out insoles, so that is what I used for the first toys. The toys I make now are felted from that lumpy hair that I can't use for insoles. Making these is kind of like ceramics - the results can be fun surprises.

Of course, catnip is also important.

For my process, first have available the following:

1. Dried fresh catnip (current year).

2. For the cases: stretchy tubes about 1 ½" wide and up to about 8" long - used old socks, pantyhose

3. Carded lumpy wool (hand cards are fine here) or: just 'wing it'.

4. Have some used plastic bags and a pair of scissors handy

5. Rubber bands or stretchy ties

With all of the above 2-5 assembled, to make the toys:

1. Wad up a walnut-sized piece of plastic

2. Wrap the carded (or not) wool around this plastic - Make sure it's all covered

3. Stuff this ball into one of the stretchy cases

4. Tie it tight.

5. Proceed with more toys - 4 or 5 should be enough (too many toys in one case makes it difficult to separate them after felting.

6. Felt the toys. Again, using the washer, soak in hot water and detergent. Process as for flat felt, but when these little pieces have begun to felt, wash them on the heavy setting for as long as it takes for them to become hard. You can't agitate them too much! Rinse at least a couple of times and spin them. When done, disentangle them, removing the ties and the cases.

7. Inspect each toy, feeling for a spot where the felt seems thin - if your plastic has a hard edge - like a bit of the closure on a Ziploc bag - that's the place where you insert your sharp little scissors and pull out the plastic. Dry the hollow toys. If you are putting them in the clothes dryer, wait to open them until they are almost dry - otherwise it may be hard to find the opening.

I usually use a dehydrator. Make sure that the insides are completely dry before you fill them. A hot sun might be the answer - my mother dried all kinds of herbs, vegetables and fruit in the sun - putting them on the dashboard of her Karmann Ghia! Try it - it works!

Fill the toys with dried catnip. If you can find it locally, great! Fresh is best. The cats know the difference. I think that each of my toys holds about a heaping teaspoon of dried catnip. I use a funnel and a chopstick to fill them.

Finish with a tail. The easiest I've found is to thread a darning needle with yarn and push the needle in from the end opposite the opening. (you may want to use a pair of pliers). Secure the yarn so that it doesn't pull out. Sew the opening shut. **Don't do a half - way job here!** You don't want cats opening the toys. Cats can be pretty determined! Have fun making these. They are very popular items.

What Else can you make with Felt Scraps?

Use your imagination. For the smaller pieces, hearts can be used in many different ways.

Angora takes dye well. Kool-Aid is perfect for hearts - use ¼ - ½ c vinegar with the dye bath - simmer until the dye is all used up. Rinse well and dry.

Cat Toys - if you want to do them that way - by using felt scraps - small kid's slippers or mukluks - I advise against making these for children who are less than a year old; angora felt sheds a bit, and you don't want a baby chewing on these. Patterns and directions in Appendix A.

Stuffed toys and/or pillows - angora felt is, for the most part, quite flexible, and it's quite easy to sew soft sculptures. A couple of things to keep in mind: 1) This felt does shed, and here, again, you don't want a child chewing on it. Also, 2) Angora is a natural fiber - one of those fibers eaten by clothes moths. (Remember cedar chests? They kept our woolen things safe from moths.) Cedar oil, patchouli and some other herbal oils or herbs can deter moths. If you suspect some damage and you can't wash the item, some time in the microwave (watch out for metal!) or a couple of weeks in the freezer will stop the incursion.

MARKETING

When one raises animals for more than one's own use, there is usually a particular focus: breeding stock, young or mature livestock, meat, eggs... with angora rabbits, you may also have a particular focus - raising breeding stock, plucking and selling raw wool, or knitting spun wool into finished angora wearables.

Probably, most angora breeders do some of each of these things. I have sold some animals - as pets or as breeding stock - and I've also sold raw wool, spun yarn, and wearable items.

When at first I tried to sell knitted items, such as caps and mittens, I sent them to a couple of specialty shops. These things remained behind glass, they could not be handled, and the clerks in charge really didn't know anything about their manufacture. Not one of these items sold. Now the Internet gives a breeder the widest customer base, but there are other good venues. Ads and periodicals that deal specifically with angora rabbits, with spinning, weaving, or felting, and those that deal with livestock and country living may bring in responses.

I have found that personally appearing at art and craft shows and fairs has been the best kind of marketing for me, my animals and their products.

There is usually some expense involved: aside from travel and lodging, a booth or space will cost about 10 percent of what you may hope to make in sales. Many of these are juried shows, and it's usually "higher end" items that are sold. If you are doing a show away from home, you need to consider what equipment you'll need to have: if it's an outside show it will be 1) A sturdy tent 2) A table or two 3) Two or three chairs 4) Display screens, 5) A spinning wheel, 6) A rabbit or two in a carrying cage, 7) Sales slips and money belt or purse with some change.

Usually at shows like that, accepting personal checks is OK. I don't accept credit cards, but if you do, this should increase your income.

I find that doing something - spinning, knitting or crocheting - will attract customers to your booth; but the rabbit is always the main attraction! Spinning with the rabbit on my lap is what I do.

If the show is indoors, you don't need all of the equipment for outside. Check with those who are sponsoring the show. Do you need a table? Chairs? Display panels? When bringing an animal inside, make sure that you provide a waterproof bottom for the carrying cage. Newspaper and plastic-coated feed sacks work for me.

For years, I have brought my rabbits and my spinning wheel to our local county fair. At our fair, we have several historical buildings grouped together in one section of the fair. I set up my spinning wheel on the "general store" porch. I find that, at the fair, moving my rabbit cage and wheel etc. on a sled lessens the amount of carrying I have to do (although there are always guys around eager to help).

Other venues for my finished items are our local food Co-Op, my daughter's cafe and Oak Knoll Acorn Studio in Amboy - also the Depot in Amboy, MN. Once in a while I get an order from someone who had purchased items from me at a rather distant art and craft fair.

I have not shipped any animals by commercial carrier. Years ago, I bought a rabbit in Fairbanks, AK. We had driven our Rambler on that summer vacation, and we were able to bring that rabbit back with us. If you need to ship an animal, contact ARBA. Rabbits are very sensitive to changes in handling and environment.

EQUIPMENT

Your equipment needs will depend upon your focus. As far as caring for your rabbits goes, you need a place to store your feed, extra water cans or dishes, and the equipment with which you clean out the coops, such as a shovel and a hoe, and then receptacles for the feed that mice and/or rats can't get into.

Equipment for using the Wool

The major equipment you'll need for spinning, is a spinning wheel.

A woman to whom I sold wool for spinning – she used a drop spindle! She sent me a photo of the lovely little jacket she'd made for a granddaughter.

The major equipment you'll need for processing felt is a drum carder. If you card 100 percent angora on anything with more than one drum, such as the larger industrial scale drum carders, you end up with little 'noils' or knots. I don't find hand cards useful for 100 percent angora.

Some time ago we bought a large multi-drum carder and a flatbed felting machine. Marlys Darnell had converted her house into a drum carding place and eventually sold us the large drum carder for $5k. The felting machine we picked up in Owatonna and paid $5-6k for it. Both worked well on angora + wool but not on 100 percent pure angora. Marlys gave me the alpaca that she'd been felting. We used that on a combination of lambswool and angora.

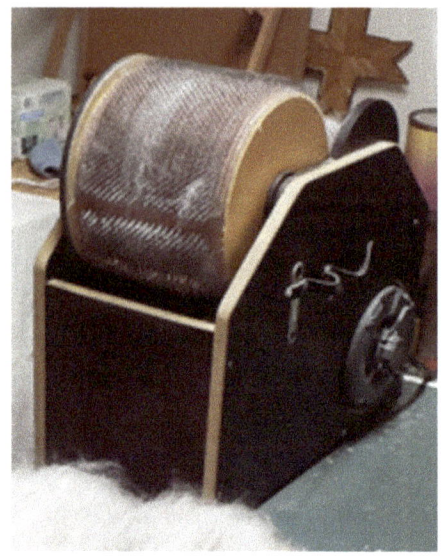

You will also need a digital scale.

Basic Healthcare Supplies

Your basic supplies should include:

Small scissors	Mineral or vegetable oil
Wire brush	Tissues, paper towels
Surgical lances	Gauze pads or clean cotton sheeting
Metal comb	Tape
Penicillin – Combiotic	Cotton Balls
Ivomectin	Dental Floss
Sulfa quinoxaline (Albon)	Small rubber bands
Oxytocin	Papaya tablets
Alcohol	Cat hairball remedy
Hydrogen peroxide	Acidophilus tablets

INDEX

A

B

C

D

E

F

False Pregnancy 36, 81, 118
Felting 21, 23, 87, 92-95, 102, 106, 107, 109, 111, 118, 134
Fly Strike 76, 77, 79, 118
Foster Care 41, 83, 84, 118

G

Gametes 31, 118
Gametogenesis 31, 118
Genetics 28, 85, 118
Gestation 22, 27, 84, 117-120

H

Haploid 31, 119
Heterozygote 31, 119
Homozygote 31, 119

K

Kindling 35-37, 118, 119

L

Litter Size 35-37, 83, 84,118, 119
Locus 31, 117, 119

M

Mastitis 42, 83, 119
Meiosis 31, 119
Mitosis 31, 119
Mucoid Enteritis 70, 119
Mutation 82, 119

N

Neutering 44, 46-48, 119
Nucleus 28, 31, 32, 118, 120

GLOSSARY

Abscesses: Localized collections of pus in tissues, organs, or confined spaces in the body, often caused by infection.

Alleles: Two or more genes at a locus. See section on *genetics*.

Alpaca: A domesticated species of South American camelid, similar to a llama, valued for its wool.

Angora: A breed of rabbit known for its long, soft wool, which is harvested and used for making yarn and felt.

Angora Breeds: Different types of Angora rabbits, such as English, French, Giant, and Satin Angoras, each with unique characteristics.

ARBA: Acronym for American Rabbit Breeder's Association.

Ashford: A brand of spinning wheels and textile equipment.

Breeding: The process of mating animals to produce offspring.

Buck: A male rabbit.

Buck Teeth (Malocclusion): A condition where the teeth are misaligned, which can cause difficulty in eating and health issues.

Building Your Herd: The process of acquiring and breeding rabbits to establish a population for wool production or other purposes.

Choosing Your Stock: Selecting rabbits based on desired traits for breeding, such as wool quality, health, and temperament.

Chromosome: The largest unit of inheritance found in the nucleus. It's made of DNA and RNA and inherited in pairs. See section on *genetics*.

Coccidiosis: A parasitic disease affecting the intestinal tract of animals, caused by coccidian protozoa.

Coprophagy: The consumption of feces, which is a normal behavior for rabbits as it helps them to digest their food more thoroughly.

Delayed Kindling: The late birth of rabbit kits, which can occur due to various health or environmental factors.

Diploid: A complete set of paired chromosomes. See section on *genetics*.

Doe: A female rabbit.

Enteric Diseases: Diseases that affect the intestines, often causing symptoms like diarrhea.

False Pregnancy: A condition where a rabbit exhibits signs of pregnancy but is not actually pregnant.

Felting: The process of matting, condensing, and pressing fibers together to create a fabric. See link to references on page 16.

Fly Strike: A condition where flies lay eggs on an animal, and the hatching larvae infest and feed on the animal's flesh.

Foster Care: The practice of having a rabbit nurse and care for kits that are not her own, often used when the biological mother cannot care for them.

Gametogenesis: Formation of sex cells in the testes and the ovaries. See section on *genetics*.

Gametes: Sex cells. See section on *genetics*.

Gene: The basic unit of inheritance. See section on *genetics*.

Genetics: The study of heredity and the variation of inherited characteristics in rabbits, important for breeding purposes.

Gestation: The period of development of the offspring in the womb from conception until birth.

Haploid: A sex cell that contains only one member from each chromosome pair. Upon fertilization, similar members of chromosome pairs unite (22 male + 22 female) = 44, the whole, or Diploid number. See section on *genetics.*

Homozygote: Identical alleles at a specific locus: The albino "cc" is an example. See section on *genetics.*

Heterozygote: A mix of genes. Mating a heterozygous rabbit to an albino will result in 50% albino (cc) and 50% colored. See section on *genetics.*

Kindling: The process of giving birth in rabbits.

Litter Size: The number of kits born in a single birthing event, which can vary widely among rabbits.

Locus: A specific region on the chromosome where a particular gene is found. See section on *genetics.*

Mastitis: Inflammation of the mammary glands, typically due to infection.

Meiosis: The process of cell division that results in the formation of sex cells. See section on *genetics.*

Mitosis: The form of division in somatic cells. The cell divides, producing two identical daughter cells. See section on *genetics.*

Mucoid Enteritis: A severe gastrointestinal disease in rabbits characterized by excessive mucus production and diarrhea.

Mutation: A spontaneous change in the structure of a gene. See section on *genetics.*

Neutering: The surgical removal of the reproductive organs in animals to prevent breeding.

Nucleus: A cellular organelle found in all body cells. See section on *genetics.*

Pasteurellosis: A bacterial infection in rabbits caused by Pasteurella multocida, which can lead to respiratory and other systemic issues.

Pets or Livestock: The distinction between keeping rabbits as pets for companionship versus raising them as livestock for wool production or other purposes.

Planning Ahead: The process of preparing for future needs in rabbit breeding and care, including housing, feeding, and medical care.

Plucking: The process of removing loose hair from rabbits by hand, particularly Angoras, to harvest their wool. See link to references on page 16.

Snuffles: A common respiratory disease in rabbits caused by the bacterium Pasteurella multocida.

Spinning: The process of turning fibers into yarn using a spinning wheel or similar device. See link to references on page 16.

Tattooing: The practice of marking rabbits with tattoos, often for identification purposes.

Tyzzer's Disease: A bacterial infection caused by Clostridium piliforme, which leads to diarrhea and liver disease in rabbits.

Wool Block: A condition in rabbits where wool accumulates in the stomach leading to digestive blockages.

Wool Processing: The series of steps involved in turning raw wool into usable yarn, including cleaning, carding, spinning, and dyeing.

Wool Mites: External parasites that infest the wool of rabbits, causing itching and discomfort.

Wry Neck: A condition also known as torticollis, where the rabbit's head tilts to one side, often due to ear infections or neurological issues.

Zygotes: Fertilized ova or egg. See section on *genetics.*

SUPPLIES

Equipment Suppliers

1. Creative Wholesales Distributors, Inc.

175 Andrew Dr. Ste 800
 Stockbridge, GA 30281
Tel: 770-474-2110
sales@creative-wholesale.com (liquid latex) Mold Builder 00795
Mold Builder is manufactured by Environmental Technology Inc, at
https://www.eti-usa.com
ETI lists the following "brick 'n mortar" distributors of Mold Builder #00795:

True Value Hardware

Local store at:

> **Main Street Hardware**
> 115 S Main St
> Blue Earth, MN 56013
> (507) 526-2876

Ace Hardware

Local store at:

> **Fleet & Farm Supply Inc**
> 1300 N State St
> Fairmont, MN 56031

Phone: (507) 238-1823

2. A hand plunger, used to wash small tubs of laundry - I used something similar to the depicted plunger, which is no longer available; The item has holes, about 20 inches long.

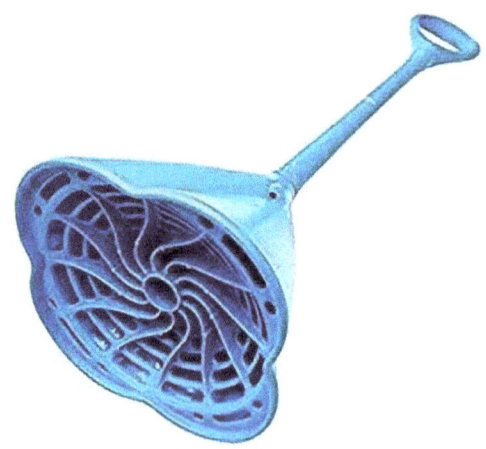

Potential alternates may be the following, some of which may be purchased online at Amazon.com:

- EasyGoProducts Hand Powered Clothes Washing Wand, Blue
- Mobile Washer Portable Clothes Agitator Brand: DayOne Gear
- Lehman's Manual Clothes Washer Plunger, Portable Breathing Washing Agitator for Bucket, Sink or Tub - Wash

SERVICE SUPPLIERS

The following are addresses and phone numbers of some potential local grooming suppliers. I don't know if they have what you'd be looking for, but they should be worth a try:

Cindy's Pet Grooming Pet Services & Supplies 2621 E Main St Mankato, MN 56001 (507) 386-1733	Hog Slat Inc 710 Cory Ln Fairmont, MN 56031 (507) 238-4448
Brummond Livestock Equipment Co 130 W Ciro St Truman, MN 56088 (507) 776-5231	Groomingdales Pet Salon 309 Blinkman St Fairmont, MN 56031 (507) 238-1881
Hen-Way Manufacturing 1807 180th St Fairmont, MN 56031-1457 (507) 436-5433	Makotah Veterinary Center Blue Earth, MN 56013 (507) 526-5516
Walmart Garden Center 1250 Goemann Rd Fairmont, MN 56031 (507) 235-2500	

APPENDIX A
DIRECTIONS FOR SLIPPERS

Directions for slippers:

Trace the slipper patterns. 'Left' and 'Right' heel pieces are the same - The toe and sole pieces will need to be flipped to have both left and right pieces.

To print these slipper patterns in the proper size, download and print the files linked by the web shortcut on page 16.

I match one end of the heel piece to one end of the toe piece. Referring to the diagram, match the X's (approximately) on the toe and sole pieces. Baste the toe piece loosely to the sole. There needs to be some "give" in the toe.

The seams should be about ¼ inch. When you've basted the toe piece to the sole, baste the heel piece - on the side which is sewn onto the toe piece - to the heel of the sole. Then you want to match the other side of the toe piece to the remaining heel side. Sew the toe and heel to the sole and the sides of the heel and toe pieces together.

To make the knitted cuff:

After you've sewn the pieces together, thread a darning needle with yarn and make ¼" blanket stitches around the ankle (The upper part of the toe and heel). When you've stitched all of the way around, switch to a crochet hook and pick up the stitches - k1, p11, or k2, p12.

When you've picked up all of the stitches, switch to knitting needles and proceed as you've begun with the first row, and make the cuff as high as you want it.

To make slippers or insoles in different sizes, start by tracing around the feet of the person for whom you're making them - leave about ¼" to ½" for the seam. You want it fairly loose. Alternatively, looking at the woman's size seven pattern, estimate how long the toe will need to be; the width will not change much - unless slippers are for some very large or wide feet. Putting these pieces together will be the way the smaller sizes are done.

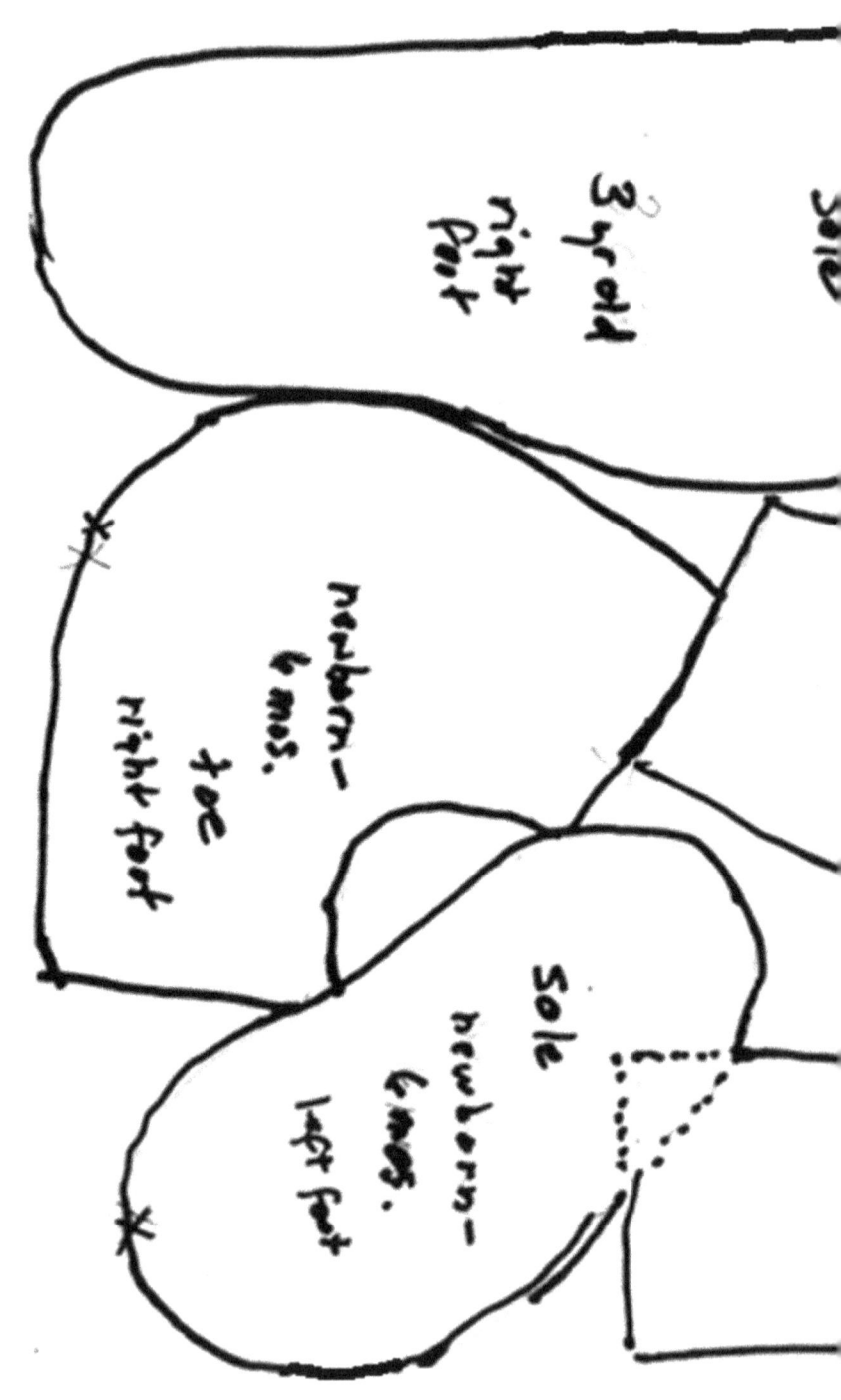

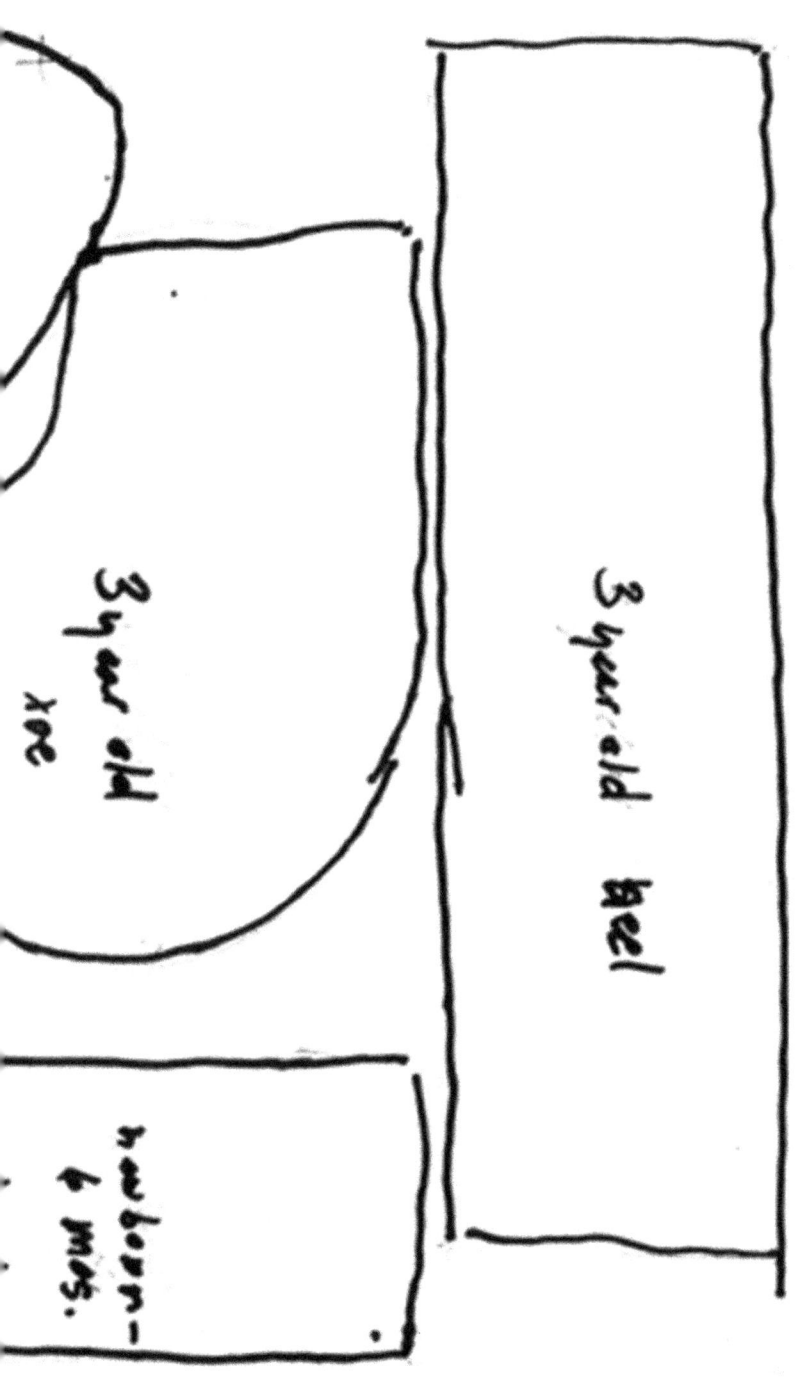

3 year old heel

3 year old toe

newborn — 6 mos.

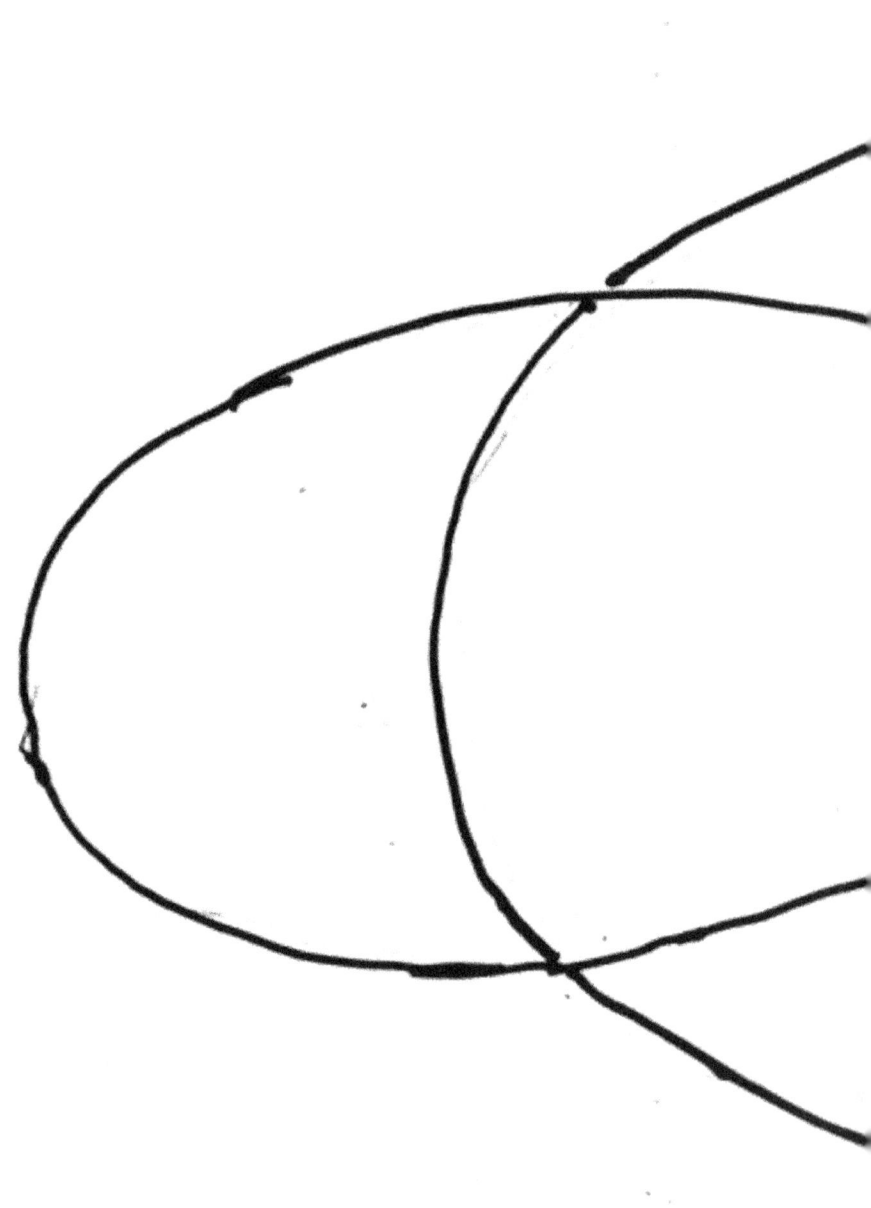

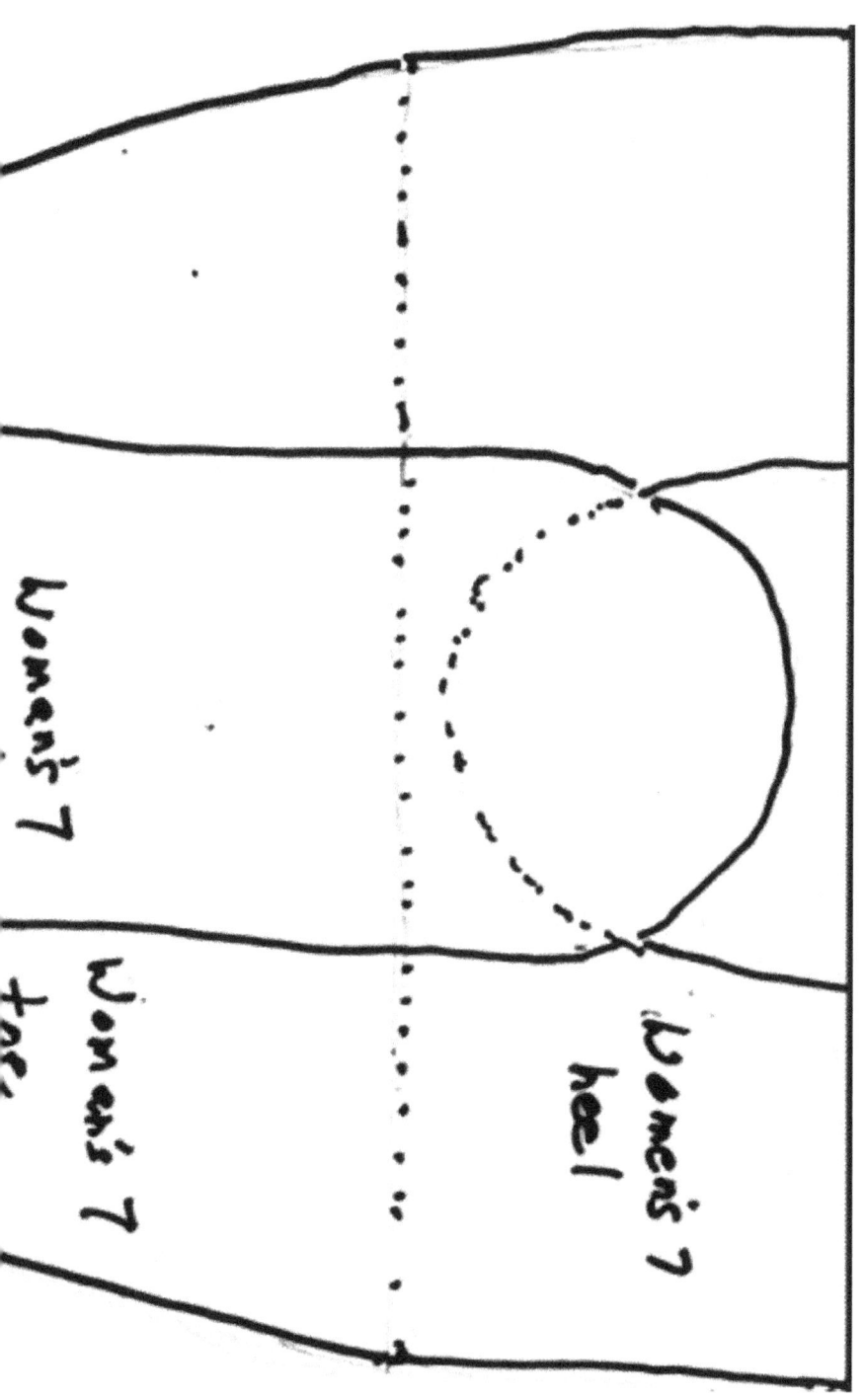

Women's 7

Women's 7 toe

Women's 7 heel

APPENDIX B
DIRECTIONS FOR MITTENS

#1 double point needles

#3 double point needles

2 oz. Angora yarn, medium fine weight

Read through "Hints for working with 100% Angora" in appendix D.

The sizes in parentheses are for a medium to large size woman's hand. This is with a stitch gauge of seven stitches to the inch across, nine rows up and down. Since pure angora mittens can be expected to shrink or felt with wear, they should be knitted with the thumb and hand about ¼ to ½ inch longer than usual. This extra length is necessary to keep them fitting comfortably. If you knit tightly, #2 needles may be used for the cuffs without much difference in appearance and fit.

Cast on 40 (44) ((48)) stitches on #3 needles. Work one round in k1 p2 ribbing. Switch to #1 needles and work for 4". Switch to #3 needles and knit one round. In the 2nd round, directly above your starting place (see illustration), increase 1 stitch, knit 1 stitch, inc. 1 stitch, knit around. Knit 2 more rounds. Inc. 2 stitches again, and knit around. Knit 2 rounds again. Repeat this for 3 more times for a total of 10 stitches inc. Knit until piece measures 2" (2½) ((3")) from end of ribbing. Put 10 stitches for thumb on holder. Cast on 4 stitches under thumb; and with 48 (52) ((56)) stitches on your needles, knit until piece is 5¾" (6") ((6¼")) long from end of ribbing. Decrease 6 times in the next round, spacing them evenly. Knit 3 rounds. Knit 2 together all around. Knit 1 row. Draw yarn through remaining stitches and pull tight.

Thumb: Put stitches from holder on #3 needle. Pick up 8 stitches from sides and bottom of thumb for 18 stitches total ((19 for largest size)). Knit until thumb is 2¾" (3") ((3¼")) long. Next row: Knit 2 tog. all the way around, draw yarn through remaining stitches, pull tight. Finish mitten by threading yarn into darning needle and weaving yarn ends into the knitting inside the mitten.

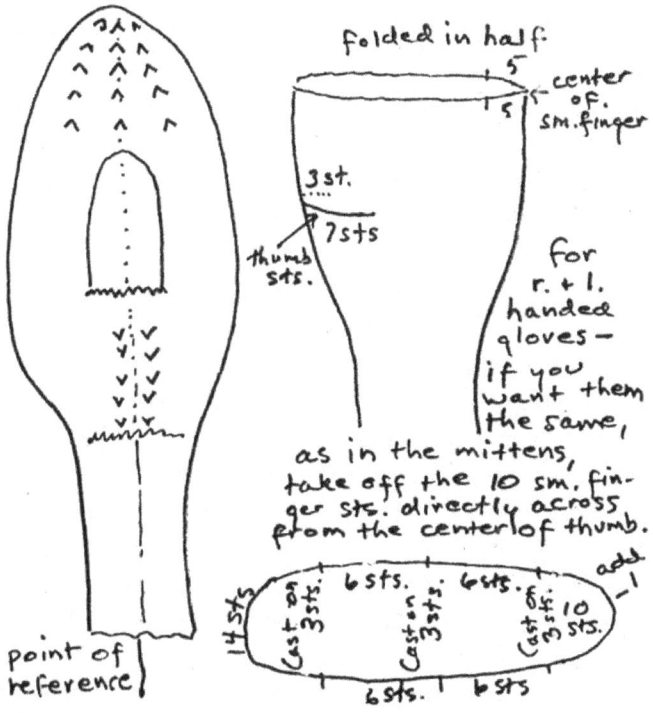

To print these mitten patterns in the proper size, download and print the files linked by the web shortcut on page 16.

APPENDIX C
DIRECTIONS FOR GLOVES

Use the same pattern as in the directions for mittens. Proceed as for mittens until piece measures 3½" (3¾") ((4")) from the ribbing. Take off 10 stitches for small finger (see illustration). Knit 5 more rounds. Take off 14 for index finger. Knit 2 rounds. Put 12 stitches on holders for ring and middle fingers. Pick up the 10 stitches for the small finger. Cast on 3 stitches on the inside of the finger, increase 1 on the side of the finger for a total of 14 stitches. Knit to 2⅝" (2 ¾") ((3")). Finish as with the thumb. Proceed in the same manner with the other fingers. Refer to the illustration for numbers of stitches. For the largest size, you may wish to add 1 additional stitch per finger. Make the ring finger an inch and a quarter longer than the small finger, the middle finger an inch and three quarters longer, the index finger ⅝" longer.

APPENDIX D
HINTS FOR WORKING
WITH 100% ANGORA

Because angora is so light, one needs less yarn. 2 ½ ounces will suffice for a large pair of women's mittens; six to eight ounces will be enough for a vest.

Since angora has very little elasticity, I use smaller needles for ribbing where the fit has to be snug. One may wish to use elastic thread in the top or bottom of some ribbing...a beret, for example.

Choose designs which take advantage of angora's unique draping qualities.

Plain stockinette stitch shows off angora to good advantage. Patterns tend to get lost in the fluff.

Avoid mitten and glove designs with a gusset between thumb and hand. This extra material simply becomes felted and pulls the thumb out of shape. For examples of glove or mitten design for 100 percent angora, see appendices B and C.

When working with double pointed needles, don't leave the same stitches on the same needles throughout the knitting process; instead, as you empty one needle, put it aside for a moment while you pick up a stitch or two from the next needle. Then start with the empty needle. The lack of elasticity in the yarn will otherwise produce "ladders" in the finished product.

Angora is a very forgiving fiber. Mistakes are literally covered up with fluff.

To clean the hair off your clothing, use wadded up masking tape, or dampened hands or brush.

Angora washes beautifully by hand. Use something like Ivory Liquid. Blot in a towel, especially if the item is large. One can lay items flat to dry, but I like to hang my smaller things on the line outside where they can blow in the wind. Angora can take a long time to dry, but with adequate air circulation or with a dehumidifier in the room where one hangs it, it dries rather quickly. Angora may be blocked with a steam iron; it may also be fluffed in a drier for a SHORT while. Make sure that the item is dry if you fluff it in the drier. Brushing with a soft brush also restores the fluff.

Angora does not react to differences in water temperature as wool fiber does.

In order to minimize felting in items such as mittens or socks, wash them frequently. Stretch them back into shape while wet. Felting does not decrease a garment's insulative quality; it seems to enhance it. Felting seems to occur mostly in items which are used hard.

Angora is a tough fiber. Hand spun yarns, in particular, are very strong, and will produce garments which will last for years - even with regular wear.

There is probably nothing warmer than angora - seven to eight times as warm as sheep's wool.

REFERENCES

SAMSON & KILFOYLE. (1992). *COMPETELY ANGORA*. Brantford, Ontario: Samson Angoras.

TEMPLETON, CHEEKE & PATTON. (1982). *RABBIT PRODUCTION*. DANVILLE, ILLINOIS: THE INTERSTATE PRINTERS & PUBLISHERS, INC.